This b

FOR

SCHOOLING

The Critical Social Thought Series
Edited by Michael W. Apple, University of Wisconsin-Madison

Contradictions of Control: School Structure and School Knowledge
Linda M. McNeil

Working Class without Work: High School Students in a De-industrializing Society
Lois Weis

Social Analysis of Education: After the New Sociology
Philip Wexler

Capitalist Schools: Explanation and Ethics in Radical Studies of Schooling
Daniel P. Liston

Getting Smart: Feminist Research and Pedagogy with/in the Postmodern
Patti Lather

Teacher Education and the Social Conditions of Schooling
Daniel P. Liston & Kenneth M. Zeichner

Race, Identity, and Representation in Education
Warren Crichlow & Cameron McCarthy, Editors

Public Schools that Work: Creating Community
Gregory A. Smith, Editor

Power and Method: Political Activism and Educational Research
Andrew Gitlin, Editor

Critical Ethnography in Educational Research: A Theoretical and Practical Guide
Phil Francis Carspecken

The Uses of Culture: Education and the Limits of Ethnic Affiliation
Cameron McCarthy

Education, Power, and Personal Biography: Dialogues with Critical Educators
Carlos Alberto Torres, Editor

Contradictions of School Reform: Educational Costs of Standardized Testing
Linda M. McNeil

Act Your Age! A Cultural Construction of Adolescence
Nancy Lesko

Tough Fronts: The Impact of Street Culture on Schooling
L. Janelle Dance

Political Spectacle and the Fate of American Schools
Mary Lee Smith with Walter Heinecke, Linda Miller-Kahn, & Patricia F. Jarvis

Rethinking Scientific Literacy
Wolff-Michael Roth & Angela Calabrese Barton

High Stakes Education: Inequality, Globalization, and Urban School Reform
Pauline Lipman

Learning to Labor in New Times
Nadine Dolby & Greg Dimitriadis, Editors

Working Method: Research and Social Justice
Lois Weis & Michelle Fine

Class Reunion: The Remaking of the American White Working Class
Lois Weis

Mothering for Schooling
Alison I. Griffith & Dorothy E. Smith

MOTHERING
FOR
SCHOOLING

ALISON I. GRIFFITH
DOROTHY E. SMITH

RoutledgeFalmer
NEW YORK AND LONDON

Published in 2005 by
RoutledgeFalmer
270 Madison Avenue
New York, New York 10016
www.routledge-ny.com

Published in Great Britain by
RoutledgeFalmer
2 Park Square
Milton Park, Abingdon
Oxon OX14 4RN U.K.
www.routledge.co.uk

RoutledgeFalmer is an imprint of the Taylor & Francis Group.
Printed in the United States of America on acid-free paper.

10 9 8 7 6 5 4 3 2 1

Library of Congress Cataloging-in-Publication Data

Griffith, Alison I.
  Mothering for schooling / Alison Griffith and Dorothy E. Smith.— 1st ed.
    p. cm. — (The critical social thought series)
  Includes bibliographical references and index.
  ISBN 0-415-95053-8 (alk. paper) — ISBN 0-415-95054-6 (pbk. : alk.
paper)
  1. Education—Parent participation—United States—Longitudinal
studies. 2. Mothers–United States—Social conditions—21st
century–Longitudinal studies. 3. Women in education—United
States–Longitudinal studies. 4. Feminism and education—United States.
I. Smith, Dorothy E., 1926- II. Title. III. Series: Critical social
thought.
  LC225.3.G76 2004
  371.103--dc22
                                                        2004009271

SERIES EDITOR'S INTRODUCTION

The language of educational reform is always interesting. It consistently paints a picture that shows what is now going on in schools needs fixing, is outmoded, inefficient, or simply bad. Reforms will fix it. They will make things better. Over the past decades, certain language systems in particular have been mobilized. Not only will specific reforms make things better, they will make schools more responsive and democratic. Of course, the word *democracy* is a sliding signifier. It carries with it an entire history of conflicts over its very meaning (Foner, 1998). The word *democracy* doesn't carry an essential meaning emblazoned on its head, so to speak. Instead it is one of the most contested words in the English language. Indeed, one of the major tactics of dominant groups historically and currently is to cement particular meanings of democracy into public discourse. Thus, under current neoliberal policies in education and elsewhere, there are consistent attempts to redefine *democracy* as simply consumer choice. Here democracy is not a collective project of building and rebuilding our public institutions. It is simply a matter of placing everything that was once public onto a market (Apple, 2001; Apple et al., 2003). Collective justice will somehow take care of itself as the market works its wonders.

As Mary Lee Smith and her colleagues have recently demonstrated in their powerful analysis of a number of educational reforms, the nice-sounding and democratic language used to promote reforms is often totally at odds with the actual functioning of these reforms in real schools in real communities (Smith et al., 2004). A significant number of things that were advertised (often the appropriate word) as making schools more responsive and better (e.g., increased testing and parental choice may serve) may have exacerbated problems of inequality.

One of the reasons this is the case is that the formation of a good deal of educational policy is actually a form of *symbolic politics*, basically a kind of theater (Smith et al., 2004). This is not to claim that policy makers are acting in bad faith. Rather, because of the distribution (or lack of distribution) of resources, tragic levels of impoverishment, the ways policies are implemented (or not implemented), and the cleverness of economically and culturally dominant groups in using reforms for their own advantage, the patterns of benefits are not anywhere near the supposedly democratic ends envisioned by some of their well-meaning proponents. (And unfortunately some reforms as well may simply be the result of cynical manipulation of the public for electoral advantage.)

In the previous paragraph, I used the word *cleverness*. Here I do not mean an individual who is able to work the system for her or his own benefit, although that undoubtedly goes on. Rather, I mean a *systemic* quality: a set of values, skills, dispositions, and propensities—what Bourdieu (1984) would call a *habitus*—that enables certain groups to employ educational reforms for their own individual and collective benefit. In order to talk about this in powerful ways, we need to talk about class.

Class does make a difference and it needs to be taken much more seriously than we have done up to now. To take one crucial example, I have argued that in a time of what is best called *conservative modernization*, one of the prime actors behind a good deal of educational policy and reform is the new middle class. Professional expertise in accountability, measurement, the generation and control of information, and new managerialism forms the basis of their cultural capital. They have occupied a considerable part of the state. A large number of new reforms in education are actually responses to and compromises with *their* particular needs and visions (Apple, 2001).

Given the increasing power of the professional and managerial new middle class, it is absolutely crucial that we engage in analyses of how they both influence, and then employ, current educational reforms to guarantee the advancement of their own children. While there are few studies of the ways in which such class fractions influence educational policies, there is an increasing body of research that critically examines how current educational reforms are used by the middle class as part of a complicated set of conversion strategies to ensure an advantage to their children (e.g., Power, Edwards, Whitty, & Wigfall, 2002; Ball, 2003). Yet ensuring class advantage takes a good deal of work. Who does this labor? As *Mothering for Schooling* demonstrates, this is very much gendered labor.

Having said that, let me situate the book even more in its larger context. There is a good deal of literature in education, sociology, and popular material that examines what happens inside schools and class-rooms that either does or does not lead to higher student achievement. At its best, the critical literature points out the ways in which the official knowledge and teaching policies and practices, as well as the testing that accompanies them, may privilege some groups much more than others (Oakes, 1985; Apple, 2000, 2001; Lipman, 2004). Yet one of the major limits of this kind of literature is that it does not examine the relationship between what happens in schools and the hidden labor within the home to guarantee success. This is where *Mothering for Schooling* enters.

We know that there are very real class and race differences in schooling. But what sets Griffith and Smith's book apart from other high-quality books is its consistent focus on the hidden gendered labor that stands behind school success and failure. They examine the hard work that mothers do and how mothers' different economic positions (middle class vs. working class) enable their children to have very different experiences in schools.

They then connect these differences back to the kinds of educational reforms that currently dominate the educational landscape. In the process, they offer a powerful critique of such reforms, enabling us to critically reflect on whether these kinds of policies will actually interrupt or exacerbate the social differences that schooling now produces. Only a focus on the intersections of, say, class and gender can illuminate why such policies and practices are misguided. This is what Griffith and Smith do.

The book is a major contribution to education, sociology, and women's studies. Because of its focus on the work of mothering in education and larger society, it has the potential to influence a number of academic areas. Not only is it conceptually and politically very interesting, but just as importantly it is written in a style that is approachable to a wide range of audiences. This makes *Mothering for Schooling* crucial reading for all of us who care deeply both about the ways in which gender and class intersect and how schools operate to reproduce and interrupt dominance.

Michael W. Apple
John Bascom Professor of
Curriculum and Instruction
and Educational Policy Studies
University of Wisconsin-Madison

TABLE OF CONTENTS

Acknowledgments   xi

Introduction   1

    The Research   2
       Downtown School   5
       Uptown School   6
    The Historical Trajectory of Inequality   8
    Outline of the Book   10

One: Women and the Making of the New Middle Class   13

    The Historical Trajectory of Mothering and Schooling   17
    A New Middle Class   20
    Women, Schooling, and the Intergenerational
       Continuities of the New Middle Class   23
    The Cycle Reproducing the New Middle Class   25
    Concluding Comments   29

Two: The Mothering Discourse   31

    Discovering Discourse   31
    Inventing the Mothering Discourse   35
    The Moral Logic of the Mothering Discourse   39
    The Mothering Discourse in Our Interviews   41

Three: Time, Scheduling, and Coordinating the Uncoordinated   47

    Constructing the School Day   49
       The School Day: Getting There on Time   49

	The School Day: Lunch Time	57
	The School Day: Coming Home	59
	The School Day at School	59
	Conclusion	62
Four:	Complementary Educational Work	65
	Complementary Educational Work: A Contribution to the School	67
	The Full-Time Housewives	69
	Educational Work As a Priority	71
	Diversified routines	78
	Flexible Routines	81
	Not Strongly School Oriented	85
Five:	Complementary Educational Work: Employed Mothers and Fathers	89
	Educational Work as a Priority	90
	Flexible Routines	91
	Not Strongly School Oriented	94
	Summary	97
	Fathers' Involvement in Complementary Educational Work	98
	Conclusion	104
Six:	Uptown and Downtown in Maltby: School and Board Perspectives	107
	Teachers	109
	Administrators	116
	Conclusion	122
Seven:	Inequality and Educational Change	123
	Education and the Changing Regime of Accumulation	127
	Changing Family Organization	130
	Conclusion	133
Endnotes		137
Bibliography		141
Index		149

ACKNOWLEDGMENTS

The research and writing for this book were funded, in part, by grants from the Social Science and Humanities Research Council (410-84-0450), the Spencer Foundation (Minigrant, 1992), and the Faculty of Education Minor Research Grants, York University. We also want to express our thanks to the administrators of the School Board at Maltby who welcomed us into their community and their offices, to the teachers and administrators of Downtown and Uptown Schools Maltby who gave their time to answering our questions, and to the mothers we talked to in both Maltby and Turner's Crossing. We are very grateful to Stephan Dobson for the precision and thoroughness of his editing and the level of comprehension and attention that he brought to the job. Acknowledgements are seldom adequate to express the kind of work an editor of Stephan's quality and abilities contributes to the final product. We would also like to thank Alison's former research assistants: Yvette Daniel, University of Windsor, and Gene Diaz, Lesley University. Finally, we want to give a special appreciation to Harvey Swanson who listened to us and cooked marvelous meals on the several occasions we hung out, writing and talking our book, at his and Alison's home.

To our sons: Rick and Mike Boulter, and David and Steven Smith.

INTRODUCTION

This book begins in our own experience. Both of us were, at the time we first started talking about doing the study, single parents with our children in school. Dorothy had been a graduate student and then a professor at a university for most of the time her children were small; Alison had been a clerical worker, a waitress in a bar, a welfare recipient while attending university, and a research associate. She went on to become a university professor. Over the period of two or three years before we decided to undertake the research, we shared confidences, complaints, miseries, and guilt arising from our relationship to our children's schools. On long walks through the ravines of Toronto, we shared the stories of our mothering work, of our children's struggles, of our fears about interfering, of pushing teachers too hard, and of not pushing them hard enough. On these walks, we also framed our collaborative research project on mothering for schooling.[1]

As single parents, we had struggled with the definitions of ourselves and our families as imperfect (they were not nuclear) families. Alison's study (1984) of the ideology of single parenthood and its role in the public school system was the first step in our long journey of discovery. She examined the theories that prevail among educators of the consequences of this *kind* of family organization on how schools can function. Educational psychology drew profiles of the problem child and held him or her to be the outcome of the single-parent family. Single parenthood created children who were problems for schools. Hence, if there were relatively large numbers in any given community, the school could not operate at the same level as in communities in which there were few. Educational policy makers at the time of her study viewed communities in which there were relatively high rates of single parenthood as needing special support and hence supplementary resources.

Out of our conversations, and Alison's discoveries, came our interest in investigating not the single-parent family, but the intact, two-parent family in relation to schooling. Alison's study established a base from which our research planning could proceed. Clearly, single parents were important to educators whether in school administration or in schools. But while the *deviant* or *defective* family was defined, and its effects on the kind of behavior of children to be expected in the classroom were specified, there was no specification of what it was about the standard North American family that was consequential for schooling. What was it about the family form in which the husband was employed outside the home with the wife doing the unpaid work of the house and childcare and with children in school that was consequential to the educational system and to the ways in which inequalities of educational opportunities were reproduced?

THE RESEARCH

Our research was a path of discovery. Looking back, we can see that when we undertook our project we were immensely ignorant of how schools worked and how schools were embedded in and shaped by educational discourses. Our experiences as mothers did not teach us about the workings of the school system, or about how our mothering work contributed to and was organized by it.

We adopted an institutional ethnographic method of inquiry, one that Dorothy had developed as a method of inquiry that would realize the principles of what she originally called *a sociology for women* (Smith, 1987), and has more recently called a sociology for people—a method of sociological inquiry open to embodied subjects in the actualities of their lives could not be gender specific. A sociology for people is located in the contradiction between people's experiences as they are active, expert practitioners in their everyday worlds, and the organization of those everyday worlds by social relations that are not fully visible from a local, experiential perspective. In contrast to most sociological theories that begin in experience, institutional ethnography does not stop with what people already know from their everyday lives. Rather, experience becomes the ground from which to explore the social relations and organization beyond the local settings of their everyday world. A sociology for people brings into view the relations of ruling[2] that enter

and shape their daily worlds, and the ways our daily experiences participate in and construct those translocal social relations. Institutional
ethnography is a method of exploring outward from the experiential
world into those social relations that constitute our experience—social
relations in which people actively participate, and yet are larger than the
experiential scope of any individual.

The method of institutional ethnography builds from a perspective
located in people's experience and in their daily lives and doings to an
investigation of social relations and organization that are present, but
not fully visible, in the everyday world. Our own experience had taught
us the centrality of the many kinds of work that mothers do in relation
to their children's schooling, and it was this that we would make our
focus (see also Andre-Becheley, 2004, 2005). Our research began by
talking with women with children in primary school, and moved from
there to discover the institutional order of schooling in which they participated and to which their work contributed. What individual families
are able to invest in their children's education is not just a matter of their
recognizing the importance of involvement as Annette Lareau's (1989)
study suggests and as the projects attempting to enhance parental involvement at all income levels reported by Michelle Fine (1993) indicate. Rather, it is the availability of women's unpaid work to sustain and
supplement the educational work of schools. Where such resources are
plentiful in a given community, the school moves toward the educational ideal of an effective learning environment for all children.

The institutional ethnographer begins at the local level, with people
who are active and whose activities frame and organize their experiences. Though the ethnography begins with local actualities as they are
experienced, it aims to penetrate into the social relations that organize
what is ordinarily conceived as the systemic or macrolevel of the social,
from the standpoint of people whose activities produce, reproduce, and
change them, and to locate those relations beyond people's experience
as these enter into and organize their lives and work. Although it is important to recognize aspects of people's lives that are not within their
control, that they are active and at work (in the general sense in which
we are using the concept of work) is already given in the procedure.
That people are active and knowledgeable expert practitioners of their
everyday lives is taken for granted by the method. Indeed, it provides the
point d'appui of inquiry, though not its destination.

Thus, our experience of our daily lives was the starting place. We
wanted to draw first on our own, and then on the experience of other
mothers, concerning the work of mothering for schooling. We drew on
the concept of *work* as it was developed by the group called *Wages for*

Housework. That group did not confine the concept of work to paid employment or to housework. It was expanded to include all those doings of people that they intend, that take time and other resources and are done under definite conditions. We started by interviewing each other, bringing into focus aspects of mothering for schooling that would easily be missed. We discovered with each other that the work of getting children off to school in the morning was clearly tied into the requirements of the school (see chapter 3) as is the more obvious supplementary educational work that many mothers of children in primary school are involved in.

We took the interview topics from those we found in our own experience. As we constructed the interview narratives with the mothers, the interview topics shifted, expanded, and became more focused (Mishler, 1986), but we were attentive throughout to the work of mothering for schooling. We interviewed women with children in primary school in two cities in Ontario, Canada. We did not attempt to select a sample. We wanted to interview only families in which both mother and father were present. (In fact one single parent was accidentally included. Her single parenthood was not known to the school.)

Institutional ethnography isn't an examination of the characteristics of populations. It explores an institutional regime from the standpoint of those involved who are active in it, however indirectly. Thus, the first stage of a study involves interviewing people who participate in such a regime to explore with them the work they are doing and to make visible in this way how the institutional regime enters into the organization of that work. A relatively small number of intensive interviews can be used to open up exploration of how those involved participate in the institutional order and thus can be used to explore an aspect of how an institutional regime is being brought into being and sustained on a daily basis. This was the strategy we adopted.

We had learned to see the issue of single parenthood as deeply imbricated with the more general issue of how inequality is reproduced through a public school system formally committed to equality of opportunity. We located differences in class by locating the schools, and finding the women we would interview through the chosen schools. We did our interviews in two cities, starting in Turner's Crossing where our research was aborted because of the resistance of the school board, and moving on to a second, Maltby, where the school board was more welcoming.

We chose two schools in each city that served either working-class or middle-class neighborhoods.[3] Our first interviews in Turner's Crossing were lengthy, ranging from two hours to six hours. Three mothers were working-class: the family income was derived primarily from hourly wages, the parents' education ranged from high school to community college, the neighborhood was well established and close to the major city industries, the houses were small, and the neighborhood school was characterized by the Board of Education as serving low socioeconomic status families. Three mothers were middle class: the family income came from salaried professional employment, the parents' education ranged from a few years of college to postbaccalaureate degrees, the neighborhood was removed from the city's industries and was well established, the houses were large and expensive, and the local school was known as one that was attended by children from middle-class families. The mother's narratives from the Turner's Crossing interviews are accounts of complex interactions between their families and the schools.

We had difficulties with the school board in Turner's Crossing⁴ so we continued our research in Maltby. The city has a similar history, population, and industrial base to that of Turner's Crossing, and the board of education in Maltby was much more open to research. Again, we selected two schools in neighborhoods that differed in social class. Uptown Elementary is located in a well-established, middle-class, professional neighborhood very similar to the middle-class neighborhood in Turner's Crossing. So too, the Downtown School neighborhood, consisting of relatively small single-family dwellings as well as hostels for homeless families, shares many characteristics with the well-established working-class neighborhood in Turner's Crossing.

Downtown School

Downtown School is in the center of the city, close to the art gallery, planetarium, parks, and shopping. The school is more than 60 years old, has three stories, high ceilings, large windows in the classrooms, and wide echoing hallways. In our Maltby interviews with educators, we asked them to describe the two schools and their surrounding neighborhood. The differences between the two areas and the two schools are represented here as they are understood by the school administrators of the municipality. The area superintendent responsible for South Maltby described Downtown School in this way:

> South Maltby and Downtown School would be considered the other side of the tracks ... It's considered to be the lower-income families, or the lower socioeconomic background. It's disenfranchised in the sense that there are no trustees elected from South Maltby. All of the trustees that sit on our board of

education, five of them are elected, and really represent North Maltby . . . South Maltby gets less staffing, less monetary considerations. There is reluctance on the part of staff to transfer into that part to work, and reluctance on the part of principals in other parts of the region to look favorably on teachers from South Maltby who transfer to their areas, because of the stigma that has become attached to South Maltby.

There are two issues of interest in the previous quotation. First, South Maltby is not only politically underrepresented and underresourced, but the teachers are not as well respected as those who teach in North Maltby. Second, the area superintendent's description of the area elides neighborhood characteristics and family characteristics. As an ordinary feature of his description, *economic attributes become family traits*. He goes on to make the following remarks:

While there are many single dwellings and duplexes, there are no high-rise apartments per se, but there is subsidized housing. The housing is generally of a poorer nature than it would be in North Maltby. Very work-oriented people, very task-oriented people, really working very hard to make ends meet and meet the mortgage and food payments. If things are going well in the school, you leave the school alone. It's when things are perceived to be going poorly that you then become involved in the school. [There is] very little interest [among parents in the area] in becoming involved in the school, or the School Advisory Committee. They support fundraising magnificently, strangely enough. Fundraising is always very well supported by the parents, but [there is] a low level of interest until students are participating in a concert, or a play [and] that generates interest and gets good parental interest.

Uptown School

In contrast to inner or center-city schools, such as Downtown School, the middle-class schools we visited in Maltby and Turner's Crossing were situated in areas of the city where larger, single family homes predominated—streets were tree lined and cars were parked in paved driveways. Uptown School is a one-story building on a quiet street. The school is approximately 30 years old, built at the same time as the surrounding suburb. Most of the children in the primary grades walk to school with their mothers or other caregivers. The school has a large number of mothers (approximately 60, we were informed) volunteering in classrooms, for field trips, in the office and so on.

Again, in contrast to Downtown School, the educators' descriptions of the families and the neighborhood link the fathers' employment (primarily) to the characteristics of the student population. The vice-principal described the neighborhood and families whose children attended the school in this way: "This is largely a professional area—doctors, lawyers, school board trustees. And the second area [the area recently acquired through school boundary changes] tends to be, perhaps, skilled trades, or manager level, or lower administrators, and so on." The profession or white-collar employment of the father is a condition for the school's higher expectations of students.

Uptown School relies on the economic and educational resources of their students' families that will teach these students "good entry behavior" (as the Uptown School principal put it), both prior to and during their school years. When those resources are made available to the school through the student, the school's educational goals can be academically oriented, as opposed to the more pragmatic goals of schools such as Downtown School.

However, at the time of our interviews, Uptown School neighborhood was in transition, and therefore, so was the school. Urban development and a declining number of students from the traditional upper or professional-class families in the school catchment area have transformed the school population. Just prior to our research, the school had begun to enroll children from the neighboring housing development across a busy thoroughfare, as well as children from apartment highrises north of the school. The principal stated:

> The school is perceived by the community as being rather upper class and the parents of the students well educated. But I think that if you did a cross section of the community at the present time, you would find that it is a good middle-class school community. We have a lot of transition in the student population, especially at the primary grade level. The old community now, the Uptown School community where the school is located, there are very few school children left within this community. [Now] they're coming from the semidetached homes and the new apartments—more of that kind of population.

We interviewed 12 mothers (six mothers whose children attended Downtown School, and six whose children attended Uptown School), learning from them about the ways in which their work was tied in to the work of teachers and administrators in the school system. Our interviews with the mothers in Maltby had to be shorter (1–1.5 hours) and more structured than those we had been doing in Turner's Crossing —we had already used up nearly a year of our grant and had to move our study along. When we had completed and reviewed our interviews with mothers, we selected topics that we wanted to bring forward with the teachers and administrators in the two schools and in the school board. We then interviewed the principals and primary-level teachers in the two schools, and assistant superintendents in the central office of the school board.

THE HISTORICAL TRAJECTORY OF INEQUALITY

In the years since the original interviews (1987–1988), we have conducted confirmatory interviews with mothers and educators, written papers, learned from our ongoing analysis and writing, and from reading other research on related topics. Our analysis expanded and deepened as we encountered unexpected issues when we worked with our data, such as our discovery of the extent to which the premises of our research were deeply grounded in the mothering discourse (Smith, 1999). This became visible to us in the course of our research on, and reflection about, what we were finding (see chapter 2). We have come to understand in new ways the complexities of the work process we call mothering for schooling. We have also come to see the immediacy of mothering work as embedded in a historical trajectory shaping the relation between families and schools (see chapters 1 and 7).

In writing this book more than 15 years after our first interviews with mothers, we looked back from a perspective informed by the research that is reported in this book and by changes in the public school system that create a different context for the kind of mothering work we describe in the chapters that follow. We discovered that we had now to understand our own experience and our researches, including Alison's earlier work on the ideology of the single parent, in a historical framework stretching back to the early years of the twentieth century, including our own experiences as parents as well as our research, and reaching forward into the time of our writing today and the projected changes of public education that are in process. As we explored further, we came to recognize the trajectory as extending back to major transitions in the organization of North American societies, including the spread and increased standardization of a public educational system.[5] The mothering work women could do in relation to their children's schooling would differ depending on the extent to which their husband's earnings made their time available. Differences in the unpaid time that women had available for their mothering work contributed directly or indirectly to the functioning of public schools as an engine of inequality. We suggest in chapter 1 that a middle-class family evolved from the early years of the twentieth century and took on a distinctive gender organization in which women came to specialize in a distinctive role vis-à-vis their children's education and their local school. Through their supplementary educational work they made a difference, not just for their own children, but in the level at which the school could operate. Gender roles in the standard North American family can be seen therefore as tied intimately to new forms of organizing the intergenerational reproduction of a new middle class.

Public education in North America was not instituted as a path to equality, yet it has been deeply shaped by that ideal. Critique and struggle have taken up its implicit promise of universality and hence of equal opportunity. Ideals of equality were joined with the social need to generalize culture, knowledge, and skills. Education could be a way for people to become informed citizens, hence capable of true participation in a democratic society, and a means through which injustices and inequities could be rectified by standardizing opportunities to learn and advance. And yet, underlying these ideals was an institutional reality that was warped by the inequities of class, race, and gender. These contradictions in education have engaged the loving and revolutionary commitment of many. They established a critical standpoint from which the deep injustices of class, race, and gender reproduced in education's routine operation could be challenged. This book is situated in that critical tradition.

Perhaps the most surprising aspect of our research was the discovery of how little we had understood about the interdependence of families and schools. As mothers and educated women, we thought we were knowledgeable about our children's schooling. As our research proceeded, we began to see how little we knew. We see our ignorance, now, as an innocence that was fostered by schools and by our own history as students, women, and mothers. We would have liked to have known about mothering work and its relationship with schooling when our children were in school. We hope that this book illuminates the often mysterious relationship between mothers' everyday educational work in the home and the organization of their children's schooling.

OUTLINE OF THE BOOK

We begin our story by locating it in the historical trajectory of education and class described in the preceding paragraphs. This trajectory (chapter 1) extends back to the previous century, to the development of mass compulsory schooling in capitalist societies and particularly, for us, in North America (north of the Mexican border). In this chapter, we reframe the topic of social class, family, and academic achievement by examining the emergence of a new class or section of the middle classes at the end of the nineteenth and beginning of the twentieth centuries in relation to the emergence of the new forms of organizing society that institutional ethnography calls *the ruling relations*. We are particularly concerned here with the emergence of a distinctive organization of gender in which, in the middle classes, women came to play a special role vis-à-vis the public school system. The availability of women's unpaid work among the middle classes contributes, we suggest, to the ways in which the public school system comes to operate as an engine of inequality.

In chapter 2, we explore what appeared to us, at first, as a detour. Our discovery and analysis of the mothering discourse was important because it opened the doors to the discursive links between developmental psychology, educational curricula, and mothering work. The mothering discourse is fundamental to the commitments that mothers, particularly middle-class mothers, make to educational work with and for their children.

Chapters 3 and 4 focus on the actual work of mothering and schooling. Our conception of mothering as work came out of the women's movement and the insistence on seeing housework as work. By analogy, in our research we conceived of mothering as the work that women do with and for their children in relation to schooling. This work is located in the social relations between families and schools—part of the organization of a social relation required to construct the particular character of an institution.

We look particularly at two aspects of mothering and schooling. First, we explore the way that family routines are themselves produced in the institutional relation between families and schools. In particular, we look at the ways mothering work coordinates the uncoordinated schedules of family members, which enables the school to operate on the tight schedules that are now a feature of public schooling. When, for various reasons, mothers do not do their educational work, or when only some mothers do this kind of work, we see how the teachers have to adapt their classroom routines and work differently.

In chapter 5, we detail the situations of women who are full-time housewives and who are able to deploy the after-school hours for educational work, and then contrast these stories with those women who are employed full time. It is clear that participation in full-time employment means that they have less time available for the supplementary educational work than those who are either not employed or employed only a minimal number of hours. We also take up what we learned from talking to the mothers about the ways in which the fathers participate in the educational work done in the home.

In chapter 6, we look at the ways that the school administrators and teachers take up differences in educational work. We look at how they organize and manage the school or classroom in the different types of communities and show how those differences are consequential for the educational and coordinative work of mothers.

In our concluding chapter, chapter 7, we revisit the historical trajectory of educational inequality. We return to our experience and that of two mothers and a father who have children in elementary school. We can see an intensification of mothering work as resources are withdrawn from schools and governments hand down the work of teaching and learning to the family.

1

WOMEN AND THE MAKING OF
THE NEW MIDDLE CLASS

This chapter situates our experiences of being single parents, our research, and our data analysis in a historical trajectory of mothering for schooling. Over time, middle-class women have come to play a distinctive part in reproducing their own middle-class status for their children through the public school systems of North America. Middle-class women's work as mothers has contributed largely invisible resources of thought, energy, and involvement to the elementary schools their children attend. Although women in lower-income groups are supportive and active in their children's upbringing and schooling, their work as mothers is done with fewer economic resources and smaller amounts of school-oriented time than those of most middle-class women. As we will see in later chapters, and as the literature on families and schools has shown, a middle-class family work organization is presumed by schools. Where mothers' work does not, or cannot, participate fully in this social relation, the family-school's reproduction of a middle class is jeopardized. We take up the problem of inequality in schooling as being produced partly *in* that relation, not external to it.

In this chapter, we argue that a characteristic form of middle-class family organization has emerged in which the male partner occupies a professional or managerial type of occupational position. In this social location, he is able to earn enough to enable his wife to stay home and to commit herself in various ways to her children's health, socialization, and to supplementary educational work supporting their schools. Unlike the research and thinking on schooling and inequality (discussed in the Introduction and below), our analysis does not explore how a middle class is reproduced in terms of the contributions families make to the achievement of individual children. Rather, we follow Ann Manicom's (1988, 1995) analysis that argues that low- versus middle- or high-income neighborhoods create different conditions of work for teachers in the classroom. Different social conditions of parenting are consequential for the school and how it can function—an effect that has far-reaching implications for all the children in the school. Manicom's reasoning is straightforward: teachers in primary schools in low-income areas have to put classroom time into educational work, or work supplementary to schooling such as teaching children how to put the yellow paint brush back in the yellow paint pot, teaching the characteristic routines of classroom learning, and providing breakfast snacks. These are tasks that, typically, can be taken for granted in middle- and high-income areas. The time that goes into these tasks is withdrawn from the required curriculum. Hence, the required curriculum has to be delivered at a lower level in low-income areas than it is where extensive supplementary educational work is done at home.

In this chapter, we address the issue of inequality through schooling in general and put forward an account of the historical trajectory of the middle classes that has established a distinctive gender organization of the family through which class position links one generation to the next. Underpinning our argument is an insistence on a conception of class as coordinated economically and socially through the daily activities of people.

The studies that examine the relationship between class, family and schooling (e.g., Bourdieu & Passeron, 1977; Coleman et al., 1968, 1993) establish a relationship between class position and schooling outcomes. Theoretically divergent approaches, such as Lareau's (1987) or Henderson's (1996), stress the specifics of the activities families do or might do that make a difference to their children's school achievement. Most studies of families and schools recommend a closer relationship, especially for minority and working-class families whose children have traditionally been less successful at school. With few exceptions (e.g., Baker & Stevenson, 1996; Hrabowski, Maton, & Grief, 1998; Winters, 1993), gender distinctions are blurred through the use of the term *parental involvement*.

Regardless of theoretical perspective, such studies agree on the importance of the family's contribution to their children's schooling:

> The evidence is beyond dispute. When schools work together with families to support learning, children tend to succeed not

just in school, but throughout life. In fact, the most accurate predictor of a student's achievement in school is not income or social status, but the extent to which that student's family is able to provide the following forms of support:

1. Create a home environment that encourages learning;
2. Express high, but not unrealistic, expectations for their children's achievement and future careers;
3. Become involved in their children's education at school and in the community. (Henderson, 1996, p. 1)

Notable among studies of the relationship between families and schools is Annette Lareau's (1987, 1989, 1999, 2000, 2003) focus on the family activities through which cultural capital is invested in children's schooling. The original concept of cultural capital, as formulated by Bourdieu (1977), dispensed with the active presence of parents resulting in the formulation of an almost mechanical relation between the system of economic production and its class structure on the one hand and the educational system on the other. Educational researchers such as Lareau have transformed this mechanistic formulation into one that argues for a more active conception of cultural capital. She notes that children whose families introduce them to a culture that is in tune with the class-based assumptions of school pedagogy and curriculum are more successful than those whose families do not. She examines parental involvement in the school, and accounts for differences in family involvement in children's schooling largely in terms of cultural differences between the middle and working classes. She notes that the interactions between families and schools are much more intensive in middle-class families than in working-class families, and argues that the intensive relationship coordinated by middle-class families with schools is one through which cultural capital is organized and invested.

In general, in the literature on families and schools, class differences are treated as already given and examined as they determine, or at least shape, the outcomes of schooling for children. The direction of determination goes from class to family to school achievement, or, in the case of the Bourdieu–Passeron model adapted by Lareau, from class to family to class culture to school achievement.

We have taken up the concept of class differently. We insist on the existence of class as active in forms of social organization. So too are we adamant about people's presence as subjects and agents who are active in those forms. We do not conceive of it positionally, whether these positions are defined by income or occupational status. Positional concepts of class run into problems once issues of gender are raised. Joan Acker (1980) originally raised the issues of gender and class many years ago; she showed that women have little presence in the studies of class and family. Deriving class position from an occupational position or from a position in a statistically constructed representation of the distribution of income levels in a society means deriving the class position or status of dependents (generally women, and invariably, children) from that of the principal earner. Thus, how class position is replicated is not recognized as a definite product of people's actions and inventions. Children's achievement in school, and hence their differential access to middle-class occupations, is treated as an effect of class mediated by family or culture or both. The approach we put forward below problematizes these effects. We want to discover the actual social organization and relations in which people are active and, most particularly, to bring into view the distinctive gender organization that is inseparable from the making and remaking of inequality through the public school system.

In exploring this problem, we have adopted an understanding of class from Leonore Davidoff and Catherine Hall's (1987) study of the emergence of the middle classes (or bourgeoisie) in Britain in the eighteenth and early nineteenth centuries. Though Davidoff and Hall work historically and without an explicit sociological framework, their study explicates the complex and dynamic development of a social organization that tied the emerging capitalist enterprise of that time into a new form of home and family and the relationships of men and women. In their remarkable study, we see the progressive differentiation of home and home economy from that of the enterprise and the constitution of a distinct domestic sphere as men and women reorganize their ways of living. Though clearly these changes are linked to changes in the development of the institutions of a capitalist economy and feed back into them, it is not possible to say just where class starts and something else (family or gender) begins. *Women* and *men* never become merely mediating terms linking a pregiven economic structure to forms of family. They are subjects and agents.

We translate Davidoff and Hall's historical treatment into social organization and social relations to give a presence, not only to the agency and activity of the men who are at work in earning the living of family members, but also to the agency of women whose work in home and family has been, and remains, so significant in the intergenerational continuities of class. Our concepts of social organization and social relations are used to locate the ways in which people's activities are coordinated, whether the forms of coordination are direct and local, or whether they are mediated by objectified relations determined by money and commodities and/or by objectifying texts. The concept of social relation is particularly useful in enabling us to start with people as they are actually located in their daily lives, and to explore how action and experience is tied into the institutional forms through which their activities are coordinated with those of others they may never see or know.

THE HISTORICAL TRAJECTORY OF
MOTHERING AND SCHOOLING

The historical trajectory linking families and schools that we are describing in this book has been laid out over the hundred-or-so years of the public school system in North America. The distinctive organization of the paid work-family-household-schooling social relation in the middle classes has produced an engine of inequality giving a credentialed, predominantly white, middle-class privileged access to positions in the ruling institutions.

At the end of the nineteenth and the beginning of the twentieth centuries in North America and other developed countries, rapid innovations were being made that permanently transformed the way in which the social is organized at the level of the society at large (Beniger, 1986). These innovations were formative of the ruling relations in North America where the sheer vastness of distances and the difficulties of communication inhibited the emergence of the strong, centralized form of government characteristic of European nations. Developments in the bureaucratization of the state, familiar in Weber (1978), were accompanied by radical innovations in the management of business enterprises and in the new form of the corporation, separating ownership and control and moving away from the identification of business with individual owners and managers (Chandler, 1977; Noble, 1979; Roy, 1997).

During the same period, there was a major movement for rationalization and reform in city government in the United States (Schiesl, 1977, p. 2). Professional city managers modeled on the management of corporations (Schiesl, 1977, p. 173) were introduced. There was a rapid expansion of educational institutions, both of the public school system and of institutions of higher learning (Darville, 1995; Veblen, 1968). Training for teachers was increasingly emphasized, and school curriculum became more standardized. Professional training in universities and colleges enabled individuals to exercise standardized competencies in multiple local sites. From the middle of the nineteenth century on, professions in general came into new prominence as a method of guaranteeing training, credentials, and standards of practice in the dispersed settings of professional practice (Larson, 1977; Noble, 1977), a development of special importance in the geography of North America.

In these developments there emerged a distinctive mode of organizing society independent of particular individuals and particular local settings and relationships; Dorothy has called this complex the *ruling relations* (Smith, 1999). Although discrete institutional forms such as corporations, mass media, government bureaucracy, and so on can be identified, the relations of ruling have become increasingly embedded in common technologies of communication and regulation, control, management, and the like. They are mediated by texts and textual technologies (e.g., print, film, radio, television, computers). The ruling relations are social forms in which *consciousness* and *agency* become objectified and independent of particular people. They have become a medium in which people act and experience and include the phenomena that we know from Michel Foucault's work as *discourse*—those distinctive genres of speech and writing, consciously developed and systematically taught, that constitute subjects and order the text-based realities of the ruling relations. They are, it must be stressed, media of action and not merely of regulation and control.

The translocal character of the ruling relations relied, and continues to rely, on formalized credentials guaranteeing competencies of a specific kind—competencies that can be seen as generated independently of any particularized relationships, for example, such as those between teacher and student, craftsman and apprentice (Noble, 1977). These new forms of social organization and relations created an ever-increasing demand for people with the kinds of skills in literacy and numeracy that depend on schooling rather than learning within the particularized relationships of apprenticeship or familial settings.

> Specialists appeared in technical fields, in sales, company and personnel management who had prepared for their jobs in specific courses of study at trade schools or colleges. Written communication increased within the firm; the number of office departments increased and with them, the number of white collar workers. Manual and nonmanual jobs, and thus blue and white collar functions, became more rigidly separated. . . . Great firms internalized many functions which had previously been performed by independent market-related institutions, for example, in sales, law, and research. (Kocka, 1980, pp. 43–44)

Kocka emphasizes the coordination of educational change with the changed demands for the staffing of management positions and of the increasingly technical character of managerial work. Such demands were not, of course, restricted to management. The translocal standardization of government administration, the professions, and education, as well as the transformation of higher education (Veblen, 1968) into the site not only of training but also of the building of the knowledge bases of the ruling relations, displaced the forms of knowledge and skills learned in the workplace under the tutelage of the skilled and experienced. The emerging ruling relations required standardization and interchangeability of knowledge and skills, no matter which educational institution an individual was trained at or where he or she might go to work. They required workers who were in touch with ongoing developments in science and technology in their field. The educational system at all levels became a central piece in the production of people to staff the rapid development of these new forms of organizing society. Changed demands on education were associated with other changes in the complex of the ruling relations; these demands intensified as these relations were technologically developed and rationalized. As they became increasingly comprehensive, they increasingly displaced autochthonous local forms of social organization.

The emergence, spread, and ever-increasing scope of the ruling relations thus involved corresponding changes of the educational system to elementary, secondary and postsecondary levels (Collins, 1979). An educated labor force, not simply educated elites, was needed. By the late nineteenth century the tax basis for general public education had been established in both the United States and Canada (Beck, 1965), and by the early twentieth century, school attendance had become compulsory (Beck, 1965, p. 89). It has been argued that the development of the United States school system was in large part driven by the perceived need to homogenize the language and culture of heterogeneous immigration (Collins, 1979; Gouldner, 1979). Schools were organized to create, *for at least a segment of the population*, a generalized level of skills and cultural background oriented to the emerging relations of ruling (compare Gouldner, 1979, p. 13), and to prepare young men for further education at the postsecondary level establishing their credentials for career-based occupations. Similarly, Bruce Curtis (1992) suggests that the establishment of the Canadian public school system is integral to state formation in Canada.

A NEW MIDDLE CLASS

The emergence and expansion of the ruling relations was the basis for the emergence of an educationally specialized class of professionals, managers, and white-collar workers who both staffed these new forms of organization and were and are active in their expansion. At the turn of the twentieth century, a new middle class emerges, distinct from the middle class of family-based enterprise characteristic of earlier North America. The new middle class is defined occupationally, that is, as earning a living through participation in the ruling relations, whether as independent professionals or, typically, as earning a salary rather than a wage, a form of employment in which pay is not related to the part played in the production of commodities.[1] Mills describes this change as follows:

> In the early nineteenth century, although there are no exact figures, probably four-fifths of the occupied population were self-employed enterprisers; by 1870, only about one third, and in 1940, only about one fifth, were still in this old middle class. Many of the remaining four fifths of the people who now earn a living do so by working for the 2 percent or 3 percent of the population who now own 40 percent or 50 percent of the private property in the United States. Among these workers are the members of the new middle class, white-collar people on salary. For them, as for wage workers, America has become a nation of employees for whom independent property is out of range. Labor markets, not control of property, determine their chances to receive income, exercise power, enjoy prestige, learn and use skills. (Mills, 1951, p. 63)

Mills (1951) includes a simple table noting changes in the percentage of the labor force of the old and new middle classes from 1870 to 1940. In 1870, the old middle class were 33% and the new middle class only 6%. By 1940 a substantial shift is visible. The old middle class are only 20% whereas the new middle class are 25% of the labor force (p. 63).

The conception of a new middle class locates the same general change in the organization of social differentiation that has been identified as the emergence of a *New Class* by writers such as Alvin Gouldner (1979) and Barbara Ehrenreich and John Ehrenreich (1979). These writers see a New Class, identified by Ehrenreich and Ehrenreich with "salaried mental workers" (1979, p. 14) or by Gouldner as the intelligentsia, becoming ascendant after the Second World War. Nicos Poulantzas (1975), while preserving the overriding dual class opposition of capitalist and worker as the primary contradiction in society, traces in his concept of the new petty bourgeoisie the same empirical region as C. Wright Mills.[2]

The new middle class emerging at the end of the nineteenth and beginning of the twentieth century in North America has grown and expanded with the growth and expansion of the forms of organization that are mediated by technologies of the text.[3] Both women and men have been, and are, active in the creation, elaboration, and transformations of institutions that were, to varying degrees, an accession to new forms of power. As forms of power, these new institutions were simultaneously limited and facilitated by the processes through which capital was becoming reorganized. The invention of the corporation as a form of organizing capitalist enterprise[4] enabled capital to take forms independent of particular local settings and particular individual owners. It created opportunities as well as pressures for the development of new institutional forms. The middle classes of the twentieth century were present and active in the invention and elaboration of institutions that transformed them from the nineteenth-century patterns of family-based small business basis (Mills, 1951; Ryan, 1981) to dependence on the various forms of the ruling relations (Campbell & Manicom, 1996; Smith, 1999). The radical changes in forms of management have been attributed by Graham Lowe (1987) to "the rise of a new professional class of managers whose quest for efficiency wrought far-reaching rationalizations in work processes" (p. 25). The innovations that have transformed the institutional order of the society in general have largely originated with, or been developed by, members of the new middle classes. This is no less true of the ways in which women as mothers have contributed to the making and development of the public school system. The women of the new middle class were, and still are, active in the social relations through which their own class position is transmitted to their children through the mediation of the public school.

The continuity of what Mills (1951) calls "the old middle class" was provided by the transmission of property combined with the skills learned in the context of familial relationships and the work done by family members contributing to the family enterprise. The nineteenth-century North American middle class was based on family; both the immediate family sharing a household, and the more extended relationships that connected an individual businessman into networks of support and cooperation (Ryan, 1981). The old middle classes were built on individually owned businesses intimately connected to family organization for the mobilization of capital and other forms of support, for the continuity of the enterprise from one generation to another, and for trustworthy management and sales and clerical staff (Ryan, 1981; Davidoff & Hall, 1987).[5]

The emergence of the ruling relations of the new institutional order created a new base and new opportunities for the middle class. Access to positions in a business enterprise was no longer largely a matter of familial connections. Now, positions in the ruling relations, whether of bureaucracy, management, or the professions, came via the awarding of credentials through a universalized educational system that included schools, colleges, and universities. Positions in a middle class were no longer inherited. No property in a position was established. The new forms of ruling organization were specifically detached from the familial (Weber, 1978).[6]

Formal credentials produced by school, university, and college became essential for admission to the new forms of career-structured employment in an organization or profession (Collins, 1979). In ensuring the transmission of middle-class status to their children, the new middle class had to rely on educational institutions that would secure the appropriate credentials. Middle-class women came to play a central role in educational institutions, although no less invisible than their previous work in the transmission of class through familial organization. In principle, the public school system was available to all, but women played a distinctive role as mothers. They were active both in creating the institutional forms schooling came to have and, as mothers, in preparing their children for schooling and for success in school. Women's work has come to play a highly significant part in the operation of the public school system as a means of transmitting parental status to children. The gender organization of the new middle class became the male parent active in a professional, administrative, or managerial job and earning a salary sufficient to enable his wife to devote her time to children, household, and the building of appropriate social connections for the family. Women's work in relation to the schooling of children has been integral to the adaptation of the public school system as a medium through which middle-class parents transmitted their status to their children.

The middle class being created in this process was for many years solidly white. The advantages that the white, English-speaking, middle-class families were creating for themselves through schooling were the basis of exclusions for others—Native and Hispanic peoples, Americans and Canadians of African descent, and the majority of working-class people (other than those few who were able to make their way through the school system into the middle class). Among African North American communities, education was a central site for struggle in which women played a leading role. While the African North American community achieved its own internal professional positions in the health professions, in education, and in scholarship, wider access to positions in the ruling relations (e.g., government, law, management, media, and so on) were radically limited until after the Second World War and are still contested. The differentiation of subordinated populations was, to a significant extent, regulated by differential access to types of educational opportunities. Access to positions of agency in the ruling relations was almost exclusively via the white-dominated school and university system, other than those that were restricted to the African North American community itself.

WOMEN, SCHOOLING, AND THE INTERGENERATIONAL CONTINUITIES OF THE NEW MIDDLE CLASS

During the early years of the twentieth century, many middle-class women became active in movements to introduce new approaches to children's socialization and education, for example, agitating for the introduction of Froebel's methods for kindergarten teaching, and pressuring for the establishment of child development as a field in colleges and universities (Rothman, 1978). In 1897, the National Congress of Mothers was founded. This group was concerned directly with schools, with furthering parental influences in them, and with promoting and supporting the establishment of local parent-teacher associations (PTAs) (Cutler, 2000). Local PTAs made it possible for mothers to be directly influential in the schools of their children (Dehli, 1988).

Until the mid-1920s the PTA movement in the U.S. was part of a wider movement for social change. Members were involved politically in the peace movement and in movements for social welfare. In the 1920s, however, the *Red Scare* in the United States was successful in making popular movements for peace and social justice politically disreputable. The focus of the PTA movement became restricted to schooling (Ladd-Taylor, 1997, p. 465). Educational experts came to exercise leadership and a more general orientation towards families and schools. For example, the National Congress of Mothers became the National Congress of Parent-Teacher Associations (Ladd-Taylor, 1997, p. 466).

The National Congress of Mothers had represented local PTAs. However it excluded the PTAs of African American women (Walker, 2000). Dedicated to the educational interests of African American people in the United States, African American PTAs were organized, in

1926, into the National Congress of Colored Parents and Teachers (Grant, 1998) that gave a national presence to many regional initiatives. In general, the interests and activism of African American women in education confronted and continues to confront the barriers of racism and racial segregation (Dickson, 1998; Higginbotham, 1985; Turner, 1990).[7] Despite the difficulties they confronted in the larger struggle for equality for African Americans, middle-class African Americans, like middle-class white women, sought security and advancement for their children through the credentials available through the public school system.

The various organizations through which middle-class women in both Canada and the United States sought to influence the school system in their favor were also the settings for their own education on how to work with their children at home to improve their children's success in school. Mothers' informal learning in these organizational settings about current trends in curriculum and pedagogy strongly supported (and continues to support) their educational work at home with their children. These organizations were foundational to the specialized relationship between middle-class mothers and their children's schooling that is the focus of our investigation in this book.

The advantage of middle-class mothering has been primarily women's economic base in marriage, which includes the everyday work of mothering that contributes to the school, *and* living in a neighborhood where there are other similarly placed families. The latter is an important point of emphasis. Our argument is not simply that middle-class mothering contributes to an individual child's achievement; that has been well documented in the educational literature. Rather, our emphasis is on how the supplementary educational and related work in the home delivered by women in a given community enables the school as a whole to function at a higher level than it can where those contributions are curtailed or absent.

Historically, a distinctive gender organization of the middle classes had emerged that, in effect, made women responsible for the work that would ensure that their children could reproduce the class status of their parents. The public school system provides, in principle at least at the elementary school level, a standardized educational program. This standardization became what we have called an engine of inequality through the addition of middle-class women's supplementary educational work to the educational work of the school (Smith, 1998). Women, who as mothers have time to dedicate to their children's education, contribute to the functioning of the school in ways that are seldom recognized as work.

THE CYCLE REPRODUCING THE NEW MIDDLE CLASS

The social relations reproducing the new middle class can be seen as a sequence or cycle—as a complex organization of social relations that includes families, and incorporates institutional arrangements as they function differentially in different relational complexes. The intergenerational reproduction of the middle class is itself an organization of class. Historically, and with few exceptions, the children of white middle-class families attended schools where they could attain credentials enabling them to attend colleges or universities. This does not mean that they had a strongly academic orientation (Coleman et al., 1966), but that they could follow a course of study qualifying them for admission to the next higher level of education in colleges and universities. White men could enter college programs that admitted them to professional careers or earn general degrees that would suffice for entry to a career in management, public service, or a profession (Darville, 1995). As they advanced, even modestly, in the career process, their earnings increased. Indeed, it seems likely that notions such as career, merit, etc., were themselves the creation of a middle class active in expanding the possibilities of these new forms of organization.

Women's participation in the social relations of class differs from that of men. Until fairly recently, white middle-class women could get high school, and perhaps university credentials. Credentials for women were preliminaries to noncareer structured jobs, such as those of secretaries, teachers, or social workers. In general, women in the work place were subordinated to men and held positions that had no career process and limited, if any, prospects for pay increases. Women who took up professional training in nursing, teaching, or social work found that this training led to positions without advancement. Until the post Second World War period, women teachers could not continue in their profession after marriage; even thereafter they were typically confined to positions without opportunities for advancement beyond classroom teacher until the women's movement of the 1970s (Smith et al., 1978). Rosabeth Moss Kanter (1977), in her study of men and women of the corporation, provides a dual view of the place of women in relation to the corporation: They are the secretaries and clerical workers whose office space is characteristically feminized, and they are the wives committed to supporting their husbands' careers in or beyond the corporation.

This bifurcation of women's lives can also be shown as two steps or stages in a sequence that is, overall, part of the cycle that produces the intergenerational continuity of the middle class. Young women could go to work in noncareer structured jobs; they could marry and so move into the next phase of marriage, a life at home and children and without paid employment. A cycle can be identified: Young middle-class women worked noncareer oriented jobs ancillary to the work of professional men; they married and bore children. As mothers, they became dependent on their husband's income, devoted themselves to their children's socialization, and, to supplementing and supporting the educational work of the school. Hence, they reproduced in their children the education required for young men to enter career-structured occupations and for young women to follow the same kind of sequence of noncareer structured work, marriage, dependency on a husband's income, and commitment to children and their schooling.

Middle-class mothers were, and continue to be, mobilized by the mothering discourse that we discovered at work in our own subjectivities at a later time and in different forms (see chapter 3). They read articles in women's magazines and in books on child rearing (Rothman, 1978; Arnup, 1994); they might well have taken psychology courses in college on the same topic. They followed the most up-to-date sources of advice on how to rear a male child[8] who would do well in school and thereafter. The socialization of children, as a practice learned from the mothering discourse, constructs the more specialized forms of subjectivity that are called for first by schooling[9] and then by participating in the moral order of the ruling relations.

Middle-class mothers might also be active in more directly practical ways in learning something about the reputations of the schools in the neighborhoods in which they might buy a house. As their children enter school, mothers might have time available to volunteer in the school doing minor clerical tasks, supplementing the teacher's classroom work, helping in the library, and going on school trips. Particularly while children are in elementary school, mothers may be active in doing the educational work (e.g., pointing to and naming objects, reading to or helping their children with their reading, helping with math homework or spelling, taking them on trips to the zoo, the library, the museum) that produces differences—not just a difference in how the individual child achieves in school, but also a difference to the school (Jackson, 1982) and the level at which the school or classroom can function (Manicom, 1988). As well, they might be involved in organizations such as school councils, PTAs, or currently, in parent advisory councils (Dehli, 1988; Lareau, 1987). When threats to merge their children's school with a school that includes a largely nonwhite student population occurs, such as those of the amalgamation of school districts, these organizations might become politically active in organizing opposition against, or in a few cases, support for such change. This is the work of mothering that is rarely acknowledged but that is fundamental to the production of a middle-class education in a middle-class school. Regardless of whether all of the mothering work is done by mothers, shared with fathers, or bought on the market (e.g., tutoring, music lessons, cultural events, and so on), this is the work that constructs and reconstructs a middle-class experience of schooling.

The schematic of the intergenerational reproduction of the white middle-class (Figure 2-1) sketches this dynamic. The latter is produced by people active in the social relations that organize the interplay between family, school, and the class status of children who, growing up, are positioned economically to become active for themselves. The diagram displays the parallel and interdependent paths of women and men, illustrating the ways that men are deeply implicated and caught up

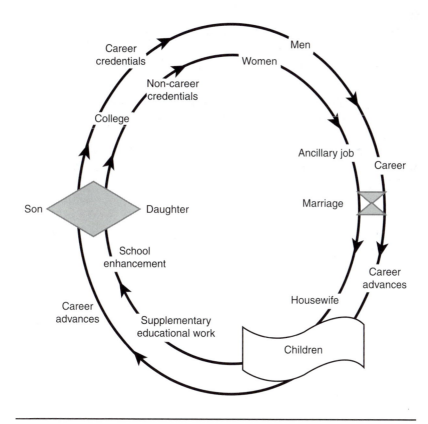

Figure 2-1 The middle-class intergenerational cycle

in their work as agents and subjects in the relations of ruling—and the counterpart processes for women, oriented to their children's schooling and linked to the ruling relations through the discourse of mothering that mobilizes and directs their efforts as a service to the school. The diagram represents the intergenerational sequences and its gender ordering, as these are connected on the one hand to the base of the middle -class family in the ruling relations, and on the other to the schooling of children.

Out of this organization of work relations between men in middle-class careers, women at home with children, and teachers in schools comes the next generation of children who will grow up with access to middle-class positions and middle-class marriages, setting the conditions for the transgenerational reproduction of the North American middle class. This social-relational process coordinating the social relations of class reproduction is essentially mediated by the universalized organization of schooling. School systems are appropriated for the reproduction of the white middle classes. It is an active process, organizing the middle classes, a process that constructs relations between family, work, and school that transforms the universality of the public school system into an engine of inequality (Smith, 1998).

Ironically, here is an intersection of gender and class—women's subordination served to sustain and reproduce, for white middle-class men, a privileged access to career opportunities in the ruling relations. Some of the gender issues that arose in the recent phase of the women's movement in North America in the 1960s and 1970s are embedded in these social relations of class.

Postmodern theory has given us a notion of the reproduction of the North American middle class, or at least a position on the subject, as constituted in discourse rather than being a property of persons. Similarly, we see agency as constituted socially. Being at work in the institutional order doesn't automatically accord agency. Despite the fact that women were the majority of classroom teachers, particularly at the elementary level, they were rarely represented in administrative positions. Men were, and still are, the majority of university faculty. Both the mothering discourse and the professional discourse of educators were developed in this institutional context. In the stories of the relationship between class, family, and schooling, women's agency in the social relations of class is suppressed in formulations that stress "*the family,*" "*cultural capital,*" or "*parental involvement.*" Thus, though women have been at work in the making of the new middle class and the institutions that sustain it, the part they have played has been less than visible.

CONCLUDING COMMENTS

In this sketch of the making of the North American middle class, we can find the contradictory intersections of the subordination of women's unpaid work to the interests of male ascendancy and male agency in the white middle class. Both men and women shared in a process of privileging the white middle class.[10] At the same time, the privileges of race and class are at odds with gender oppression, a contradiction that cannot in a simple way be generalized to minorities or to the working class, whether white or not.

Both men and women of the middle classes were at work in taking advantage of the new possibilities emerging in North America at the end of the nineteenth century. The very institutions through which their own class position and that of their children were secured were also, to a significant degree, of their own making. The very dynamic in which women played an active part, over time, came to narrow and subordinate them to the demands of service to their husband's careers, and through their service to schooling, to their children's advantage in schooling. This is an ongoing production in which women have played a central part. Middle-class women working in the interests of their children, particularly their male children, have been, and still are, active in producing those inequalities in a public school system that serves middle-class interests in privileged access to career opportunities in the ruling relations.

We have situated our research on mothering for schooling in this historical trajectory of the family-school relation. Our data represent a moment in the social relations organizing the intergenerational reproduction of the forms of inequality differentiating an educated middle from the working classes. In our final chapter, we will return to this historical trajectory from the perspective of recent changes to education. In the next chapter, we discuss the development of the mothering discourse so essential to shaping women's mothering work for schooling. The social relations of a mothering discourse can be seen as integral to the organization of a middle class, and particularly to the mobilization of women to sustain their children's special access to middle-class occupations. The historical roots of the discourse of mothering, in which our own lives and indeed the terms of our investigation had been embedded, opened into a historical moment in which the making of a middle class was going forward.

2

THE MOTHERING DISCOURSE

In devising this project and in its conduct, we consciously included our-selves and our experiences. We drew on our experiences as mothers and a common knowledge of typical school situations and problems to es-tablish rapport with the women we were interviewing. We used phrases such as: "When my children were small, I . . ." or: "When the teacher called to discuss problems, I often felt. . . ." This was, in part, a princi-pled methodological matter adopted in recognition of our own histor-ical presence in the research process, and an untheorized, ordinary responsiveness (Oakley, 1974). In contrast, when we talked with educa-tors about our research, our experience as mothers did not serve us in the same way. Instead, our focus on mothering work often provoked stories of problem mothers and their children. In this chapter, we ex-plore our connectedness with mothers and our disconnected experi-ences with educators through an analysis of the mothering discourse as it is coordinated with public schooling.

DISCOVERING DISCOURSE

The mothering discourse came into view for us first in our interview-ing. At times, interviewing mothers was emotionally exhausting for us, often provoking feelings of guilt and anxiety. Typically, these feelings appeared in interviews with women who were full-time mothers and wives with professional husbands and plenty of time to do things with their children, such as going to plays and museums. As we listened to women tell us about their mothering work, we also silently reflected on our experiences in the light of theirs. Sometimes this was painful. Sometimes our own mothering practices compared unfavorably with a mother's account of her work. Sometimes feelings of guilt were evoked —the feeling of having done our own mothering inadequately.

Talking with other mothers about their work as mothers in relation to their children's schooling revived concerns about our own mothering which had never fully subsided. Neither of us had had enough time to spend with our children going to plays, museums, and concerts. That was entirely reasonable and practical in our circumstances of time and resources. While our guilt was unreasonable, it was nonetheless sometimes acute. For example, while writing up the field notes after one interview, Alison became aware of how she was comparing her own experience with that of Marie Fisher, a mother whose mothering work was extensive and rich in social and economic resources:

> Marie Fisher has two children; one child is in the French Immersion Program at a primary school in a middle-class area, and the other is 4 years old. The mother has an advanced degree and her husband works in an academic institution. She does not work outside the home. Her interview described the extensive time and energy she spends on her children; for the time being she considers them her job. She organizes car pools so that they are always supervised during their community activities. She takes them to Stratford to the Festival. The children, who are already familiar with some of Shakespeare's plays, help to choose the ones they will attend. Marie is active in the Home–School Association and any problems that arise in the classroom are taken up without delay with the teacher and the principal. (Alison's field notes)

This account of Marie Fisher, drawn from field notes, might make many mothers feel inadequate. It certainly did us. Her mothering stands in strong contrast to our experience of being sole-support parents and, in Alison's case, living on an inadequate income. Alison went on to describe her response to Marie Fisher and to compare her mothering work with her own:

> And where was I in all this? I was feeling that I hadn't done my own mothering properly. I had let my children watch TV; they'd never been taken to a Shakespearian play; when I was upset with the school, I had never managed to make things better for my

children and indeed, at times made it worse; etc. In other words, my mothering, in relation to other women's mothering, appeared to be less than adequate on almost every count. As a consequence, I was finding the interview process very difficult emotionally.

We can see in this a familiar procedure; there were very good reasons why Alison's mothering practices were different from Marie Fisher's. She lacked her parenting facilities, time, and opportunities. But characteristically, this did not excuse Alison, did not remove her sense of guilt. The ideals of mothering in the context of schooling, and the mother's responsibility for realizing them, are absolute. The practicalities of the contexts and conditions of mothering do not appear to modify the interpretation of mother's responsibility for her child's schooling.

Reflecting on experiences of this kind showed us a strongly moral dimension governing the relationship of mothers to the school, capable of generating an almost theological sense of guilt and anxiety. We did not turn to psychological interpretations or to the kind of interviewer's stoicism that Dorothy's graduate training had insisted on (e.g., "Forget reservations, dislike, anxiety. Speak the interviewing script!"). We began to examine the social relations in which such experiences of guilt and anxiety arose. We discovered a discourse that we have come to call *the discourse of mothering* that mobilizes the work, care, and worries of mothers in relation to their children's schooling.

By *discourse* we mean a systematically developed knowledge, morality, and set of values that are expressed in definite ways of writing and speaking. *Discourse* is an ambiguous term, coming into specialized use in the 1960s in linguistics as that discipline redefined its phenomenal universe from the single sentence to stretches of talk or writing (Schiffrin, 1994, p. 23). More recently, particularly since Michel Foucault's work became widely read, it has come into general use, bringing into focus distinctive patterning of styles, vocabularies, linguistic conventions, and so on (e.g., Jary & Jary, 1991; Rosenau, 1992; Walkerdine, 1986; Weedon, 1987). As Diane Macdonnell (1986) defines discourse, it resembles Bakhtin's (1986) *speech genres*. "Discourse is social," she writes, "the kind of speech proper to the shop-floor of a factory conflicts with that of the boardroom. Different social classes use the same words in different senses and disagree in their interpretation of events and situations" (pp. 2–3).

There is a distinction to be made between speech genres that are characteristic of definite forms of social action (e.g., the shop-floor or the school playground) but that do not exist in the specialized forms in which action and relations are in language (or in numbers) differentiated from other forms of action and mediated by written and printed texts. Michel Foucault (1981) uses the term *discourse*, for the most part, in the latter sense. It is useful to think of his conception as of a kind of conversation among authors or speakers that is mediated by written or printed texts. Such conversations constitute "a conceptual terrain in which knowledge is formed and produced" (Young, 1981, p. 48). Discourses create a world in common for those who participate, constituting objects that exist independently of their experience of particular local settings. Foucault's conception has been most influential in treating issues of knowledge and truth as effects of the rules and practices of inclusion and exclusion. Hence, rather than knowledge and truth being thought of as independent of particular regions or historical periods, they are understood as specific to the discourses of a given historical period (Foucault, 1981, p. 60).

In this book, we use the term *discourse* somewhat as Foucault does, though we want to supplement it by remembering that though the author is herself a construct of discourse, a discourse does actually relate people who write, read, hear, or speak. Discourse is, in our usage, essentially mediated by texts of various technologies (print, film, computer, and so on). Texts are forms of signification linking language and consciousness to the social relations of power in society (Smith, 1990a, 1990b). Social institutions, such as education or the family, are located in and structured by different "discursive fields" that "consist of competing ways of giving meaning to the world and of organizing social institutions and processes" (Weedon, 1987, p. 35). The notion of *discourse* that we work with here shifts from discourse conceived as simply forms of signification or meaning to emphasize discourse as the local practices of translocally organized social relations.

As we use the concept here, discourse is people participating actively and embodied in a conversation mediated by written and printed materials. Each discourse has its own distinctive organization of authorities, means of dissemination, educational and knowledge-producing sites and production processes, and so on. It does not consist only of statements. It also involves ongoing interchanges between those doing research and theories developed in the context of universities and similar sites that inform, for example, media stories and child-rearing manuals. Some discourses, however, are intimately linked through particular institutional relations, for example, the mothering and educational discourses. The educational discourse provides the working language coordinating teachers' classroom experience with that of other educators and administrators. It also provides material for the writing of newspaper stories and materials for women's magazines, and links the preparation of courses in high school and colleges to practices of reading and learning on the part of professional and lay practitioners (mothers), and so on. Though our conception of mothering discourse points to the same phenomenon that Annette Lareau refers to as "a *dominant set of cultural repertoires* about how children should be raised" (Lareau, 2003, p. 4, italics in original), we have preferred a conception that recognizes a mothering discourse as the creation of professionals, popularized in a media aimed systematically at women and designed to coordinate the mothering work done in the home and the work of educators in the public school system.

As we are using it, *discourse* does not just refer to the texts of this conversation and their production alone, but also to the active ways in which people attend to, name, and interpret their own and others' doings in relationship to them.[1] As mothers orient towards the texts mediating the mothering discourse (whether in books, women's magazines, television, radio, or by participating in second-hand textually organized processes such as courses, church meetings, etc.), as they do their work in relationship to their children's schooling, as they measure what they do in terms of its standards, and as they interpret and orient to what other mothers do in these terms, they are participating in this discursive process.

Thus, the paradigm of the ideal mother constructed in relation to her children's schooling, the operation of invidious comparisons among mothers, our own recognition of ourselves as defective mothers simply by virtue of our being sole-support mothers, and the curious moral structuring of responsibility for the child's behavior in the school unsupported by corresponding control or guaranteed means and conditions, are moments in the practice of a discourse through which the educational role of mothers has been, and is still, coordinated with that of school. The duality of our own experience, as representatives of the discourse to the mothers we interviewed and as mothers ourselves, becomes visible as a feature of discursive organization into which we are entered as subjects in the two different positions within the discursive organization of mothering (Griffith, 1998).

INVENTING THE MOTHERING DISCOURSE

Our original research was done at a transitional period when radical changes in the institutional order were emerging. This involved a major retooling of the ideological and discursive resources complementing and sustaining changes in economic organization (see chapter 6). Analogously, the discourse of mothering that originated towards the end of the nineteenth century (Davin, 1978; David, Edwards, Hughes, & Ribbens, 1993) was also part of the reworking of institutions responding to the changes in the organization of economy and polity. At that time, and in the early twentieth century, as we have described in the previous chapter, women of the middle classes promoted child development as a field of specialized study and research in universities (Rothman, 1978), introduced European innovations in the education of young children, and, as described in the previous chapter, created parent-teacher organizations (Cutler, 2000; Dehli, 1988; Ladd-Taylor, 1997). The parent education movement was key to developing psychology as the theoretical ground of educational theorizing (Walkerdine, 1984). The development of an academically based discourse of child development supported and legitimated the parent education movement: "The status of the parent education movement was heavily dependent on its purported foundation in scientifically controlled observations of children in laboratory and nursery school settings" (Schlossman, 1981, p. 276).

The child development discourse originates in and coordinates the work of professionals—child psychologists and psychiatrists, social workers and educators, and authors in the popular press and television. Through the work of these professionals, the child development discourse normatively structures the limits and possibilities of our knowledge about children's maturation. As such, it forms the lens through which educators and social service professionals evaluate the work of mothering in the family. It also informs mothering work, subordinating mothers' experiential understanding of their children to the generalities constructed within the ruling relations of the child development discourse.

The psychological literature on children's development was well established by the 1930s (Richardson, 1989). This discursive conception of childhood is the substantive ground of child psychology and the basis of curricular, pedagogical, and educational assessment practices in the schooling process—child-centered education (Griffith, 1984; Walkerdine, 1984; Walkerdine & Lucey, 1989). The child development discourse is textually organized and conceptually linked to the discourse on child-centered education and to the discourse on mothering (Griffith & Smith, 1987). The dual emphasis on individual development and environmental influence, linked to empirically derived normative developmental rules, brings the family and the school into the equation in unprecedented ways.

The texts of the child development discourse are interdependent: one set of texts (e.g., developmental psychology) is the empirical and theoretical basis for other related, but distinct, sets of texts (e.g., primary level curriculum, or advice to mothers in popular magazines). The discursive regulation of our knowledge about children produces "the possibility of certain behaviors and then read[s] them back as true, creating a normalizing vision of the natural child" (Walkerdine, 1988, p. 5).

The links between the child development discourse, the mothering discourse, and the education discourse were organized through a number of social sites. A major site for the textual organization of the mothering discourse is the literature that advises mothers on their children's development (Ehrenreich & English, 1978).[2] The twentieth-century advice literature translates the findings of child psychology into magazine columns, tracts on child rearing, and popular books read by many first-time mothers. The mental hygiene movement of the early twentieth century coordinated public health and educational policy, and of course, mothering work. Schools were sites not only of monitoring children's health but also of educating mothers. Public health nurses working in the school and educational staff checked students' personal hygiene (Richardson, 1989). The mental hygiene movement and the parent education movement drew on a scientific discourse relating children's health, education, and mothering (Manicom, 1995).

Robert and Sylvia Lynd's (1927, 1937) two studies of a Midwestern community in the United States were done ten years apart. They mark a watershed in the transition from mothering practices learned from a senior generation of women to mothering practices mediated by the texts of the mothering discourse. In the earlier study, women were only just beginning to learn mothering from authorities—nurses, government pamphlets, and so forth—rather than from their mothers, elder sisters, aunts, and other women of experience. In the later study, the conversion to the texts of the mothering discourse appears to be complete.

After the Second World War, authors of child-rearing manuals "began to incorporate scientific information from the field of psychology" into their advice tracts (Weiss, 1978, p. 39). The mothering discourse focused increasingly on the mother's role in the child's psychosocial development. How mothers related to their children came to be held to make the difference between the possibilities of the child reaching his or her full potential and the social waste of his or her unrealized development. What was claimed as scientific knowledge of children's development prescribed a particular version of child rearing, hence of mothering. Children require *more* than physical care. They also require social, emotional, and cognitive care through developmentally organized activities that can facilitate their maturation. The responsibilities demanded of mothers, and the work required of them, increased as the relationship between family and school strengthened. Walkerdine and Lucey (1989) note the blending of pedagogy and mothering work implicit in the popular conception of the *sensitive mother*:

> A feature of the sensitive mother, then, is that her domestic life is centered around her children and not around her housework. The boundaries between this work and the children's play have to be blurred and so it comes as no surprise that any household task can transform itself into the basis of domestic pedagogy. (Walkerdine & Lucey, 1989, p. 20)

Proper mothering became dependent on the experts, those whom Eyer (1996) calls the "baby gurus" (p. 4), as conceptualizations of children's maturation permeated the psychological and psychiatric discourse. John Bowlby's work in Britain insisted on the mother's constant presence as essential for the infant's and small child's psychological health. Schizophrenia and other mental health problems were viewed as originating in *faulty mothering*. Popular writing on childcare followed the same line. The original Dr. Spock's *Baby and Child Care* treated the infant's relationship to the mother as having almost exclusive importance in the child's healthy psychological development, as did Bruno Bettelheim's column during the early 1960s in *Redbook* magazine (Eyer, 1996).

The 1950s also saw an increase in studies, mostly by sociologists, that linked the intact or normal family with the school achievement of children. Linkages between the "Standard North American family" (Smith, 1999) and children's school achievement were made explicit. Coleman's (1966) major study exploring the relationship between the intact family and school achievement suggested that family background was more significant than the school for a child's success. From Britain, Maurice Craft's collection of studies of family, class, and school achievement also emphasized in a variety of ways the significance of the normal family— husband, wife, and children—in the child's school career. The standard North American family was the paradigmatic form within which the healthy, successful, and (usually) male child developed. The single parent family, as Alison's doctoral study (1984) demonstrated, and as we ourselves experienced, was automatically defective and automatically transmitted problems to the children of single parent families in the school classroom.

THE MORAL LOGIC OF THE MOTHERING DISCOURSE

The mothering discourse has a characteristic moral logic. It is well described in Arnup's study of what we are calling the mothering discourse in early twentieth-century Canada. Here she describes the characteristic way in which the mothering discourse attributes blame to mothers:

> Children's behavior problems were attributed to errors on the mother's part. While the specific nature of her failings changed over the course of . . . decades, her responsibility remained constant. . . . In the 1932 edition of *The Normal Child*, Alan Brown reminded readers that "the mental environment of the child is created by the mother. This is her responsibility and her opportunity." These words were echoed in countless publications throughout the period. A 1936 article in Chatelaine [a Canadian women's magazine] warned mothers that "your child mirrors you and your home; if your child is a problem child, it is probably because you are a problem mother." (Arnup, 1994, pp. 150–1)

The mothering discourse makes no concessions to variations in the practical and material contexts of mothering work or to the realities of a mother's ability to control the school situation in which her child works during the day. Exposure to guilt, invidious comparisons, and anxiety all are constant hazards for mothers participating in the discourse. The child who does not read on time, who does not behave in ways which fit the classroom order established by the teacher in conjunction with the particular groups of students, who does not work well with her peers, or who is going through a difficult time for whatever reason, invites—via the discourse—her mother to scrutinize her own mothering practices for what is wrong.

The discursive representations of mothering have changed over time from the Victorian *good mother* to the *Supermom* of the late twentieth century (Eyer, 1993, pp. 65–67). In all its varieties, the mothering discourse has this in common—it requires the subordination of women's unpaid labor and the conditions of her life to the ill-defined needs of her children's development and of their schooling. Whereas formerly, as we have seen, women might have learned mothering in a family tradition or community from older women, the mothering discourse sets up the professionals as authorities. Psychologists, experts in child development, and social scientists became the sources of information on the forms of mothering conducive to a child's successful development. The professional educators who have taken charge of her child became the decisive evaluators of a woman's success. If a woman wanted to know what would help children to succeed in school, she would have to look for professional sources of guidance. We were caught in a circular trap: a child's success in school was proof that we had been successful as mothers and conversely, a child's problems in school demonstrated our inadequacies as mothers.

In these ways, the discourse of mothering mobilized women, particularly middle-class women, as mothers to support the educational work of the school with their own work; to be performed under a variety of unspecified conditions. The child's dress, health, regularity of attendance, social behavior in the classroom, and scholastic performance referenced the mothers' work behind the scenes. The mothering discourse located her responsibilities as a mother; the educational discourse, as we shall see later, interpreted or read off the virtues of a family and particularly a mother from the child's appearance and performance in the school setting. Being successful as mothers meant being attentive to schools and teachers; this dynamic legitimated the authority of the latter.

In these ways, the mothering discourse supports a standard family organization: the complete nuclear family. It provides systematically developed knowledge, recommendations, systems of categories and concepts, and above all, for mothers, a moral logic of responsibility that subordinates those who participate to a universalized public educational system and the family. *Above all, it promotes the responsiveness of parenting practices to educational requirements.*

The nonspecific and generalized responsibility of mothers as defined by the mothering discourse permitted, and continues to permit, as we discovered, no practical considerations to limit that responsibility. Lack of resources, time, or skills could not be claimed against it. As we had discovered for ourselves, the discourse of mothering did not recognize that mothering is work; taking thought, time, effort, and resources. The responsibilities and standards of a mother's achievement did not vary with the real conditions under which her work was done. The instructions and guidance provided in the texts of the mothering discourse are invariable across the board. For example, in a pamphlet put out by the Ministry of Education in Ontario, mothers of elementary school children were instructed to: "Have a place where your children can paint and crayon or cut-and-paste without having to worry about making a mess; spend time examining photographs and works of art with your children; and, with home-made puppets have them create plays which mother watches" (quoted in Smith, 1987, pp. 168-9; see also chapter 6 of this volume). The pamphlet takes for granted that all mothers have access to resources such as paints and papers, photographs of art, the materials for homemade puppets. More importantly, the availability of a woman's time to do the mothering work is simply taken for granted—time to clean up the mess after painting, time to sit with the child and talk about works of art (as well as time going to the library to get the picture book), time to make puppets and time to sit and watch the children put on theatre. Similarly, every Fall, at least one of the Toronto newspapers offers mothers of children about to begin school excellent advice on what to do to help the child make the shift from home to school. One such article recommends a visit to the school each day of the week before school starts, a possibility that is clearly not practicable for women who are in full-time employment. As Walkerdine and Lucey (1989) note, when mothers are engaging in pedagogic tasks with their children, they are not doing housework or paid work.

THE MOTHERING DISCOURSE IN OUR INTERVIEWS

As may be obvious, though we were critical of the schools' expectations of parents, the problematic of our original study was generated by the mothering discourse and its idealized image of what Dorothy (Smith, 1999) has called the "standard North American family." We wanted to know what was so special about the standard North American family that made it so important to schools. And though our ethnographic strategy enabled us to talk to women about how they went about the work of mothering for schools, the focus of our questions was deeply influenced by this concept. As described earlier in this chapter, we discovered the mothering discourse in the course of reflecting together on Alison's experience of how it had affected her after an interview that elicited unfavorable comparisons between the respondent's and her own practices of mothering. It was deeply built into the design of the questions we asked of respondents. A really successful interview builds relevance for interviewer and respondent. Each subsequent question fits into a sense of relevance already developed and being elaborated upon in the conversation. The frame of relevance already built appears typically in the respondent's afterthoughts when the interview is over. When the interview is concluded and the tape recorder turned off, the respondent will start generating all kinds of material relevant to the research interest. That relevance is, of course, a product of both questions and how they're taken up.

Sometimes, however, relevance does not get established. In one of our interviews in Maltby, Dorothy talked to a woman for whom our line of questioning didn't seem to connect—probably every researcher doing interviews has had this experience. Dorothy had had that experience previously when interviewing her mother about what had led her to become active in the women's suffrage movement in England in the late nineteenth and early twentieth centuries. That interview did not go well. Dorothy's mother was happy to talk, but every question Dorothy asked seemed like an interruption in her mother's train of thought. Later, preparing to teach on the women's suffrage movement in a women's studies course, Dorothy learned enough of the context of her mother's experience to account for why her questions had not made sense to her mother. Her experience interviewing Carol Irwin was also like that. The questions she asked did not come together with Carol's focus. Though Carol seemed to enjoy being interviewed, was interviewed twice (partly because of Dorothy's feeling of dissatisfaction with the initial interview), and all our questions were responded to fully, Dorothy could not escape the feeling that each next question brought Carol's train of thought to a halt.

Looking back, we can see how that dialogue and all the others were organized by Dorothy's unthinking use of the mothering discourse to frame her questions. We suspect, however, that Carol did not participate in that discourse in the same way. For her, the schooling of her daughter did not take a central place in how she organized her life; she did not feel that it was important for her daughter to be at school every day or to get to school on time. She was not in the least apologetic about this. On the first of two interview visits, her daughter was at home. She was not sick. She simply had not gone to school. At one point the phone rang and Carol, without a glance at Dorothy, called to her daughter, "Don't answer it! Don't answer it! It may be the school!" Anyone participating in the mothering discourse, however minimally, would have already explained to the interviewer why a child was at home and given good reason. Carol did not. The failure to connect, of course, was ours —or in this case, Dorothy's. She knew that there was a problem but not what it was. It is, of course, from just such failures that the researcher learns as much, if not more, than from her successes. Discourse offers a language that is both enabling and restricting. It interprets situations, defines objects, locates our own subjectivities in relation to them, and subordinates us to its moral logic.

Our research meant talking with mothers about their work, and of course, the mothering discourse entered into our talk as it had into our conception of the project. We can find it at work at many sites in the transcribed interviews, for example in our interview with Janie Apple. Janie is a nurse who worked at a hospital in her neighborhood. Her husband was laid off from a middle management position and had to take up a sales position at a significantly lower level of pay. So she has to have paid work. She is on shift work and the hours make childcare and babysitters a constant juggling act. Our interview was working its way topically through the school day, arriving finally at the after-school hours. At this point she told us apologetically that she tried to keep up with reading to the children every night—the paradigmatic reading routine of the mothering discourse—but when she is on graveyard shifts, she is not able to manage this. The demands of her job interfered with regular reading, so she made excuses: "No, I'm really a basket case on nights. I just don't have the energy or whatever to read to them or do anything with them . . . " By implication, if she could only muster up more energy she would still be able to meet the standards she ought to be realizing. The conditions of her paid employment, of the level of her husband's earnings, of the lack of adequate childcare facilities, and so on, are discounted.

Here, the mothering discourse can be recognized in the organization of our conversation, shaping the way Janie tells her story. We have direct access to the social organization of the relations we are exploring. We see the disjuncture of control and responsibility—Janie has to work and has only been able to get shift work, but she is still responsible for putting in the full complement of time into the supplementary educational work that is normative for mothers. The categorical character of the standards takes no account of practicalities and conditions. The standards are organized extralocally in a discourse on parenting and child development that sets up the parameters for normal child development and the parenting required to develop and maintain that normalcy (Chambouredon & Prevot, 1975; Griffith, 1984.) It is an organization of relations beyond the local settings of our interviews, ourselves as interviewers, and the particular women we talked to. Alison's responses to the woman whose children chose the Shakespeare plays they wanted to see at Stratford is an enactment of this dialogue between the idealized discursive mother and the real conditions of doing the work of mothering that she confronted.

Differences in participation in the mothering discourse in the different school sites of our study recreate the social relations built by the sequences of action, coordinating the work of mothers with the work of school and with the social relations of class. Here are two examples from Turner's Crossing. In these, we are able to observe differences in how those we interviewed were oriented to the mothering discourse.

Anne Dexter's children attended a school situated in a working-class area in Turner's Crossing. Also in Turner's Crossing, Desi Evans's children attended a school situated in a predominantly middle-class district. These Turner's Crossing mothers were actively involved with their children's schools and teachers in a variety of ways—both volunteer at their children's school, and go to every report card conference and to all the school events. However, they talked very differently about their children's schooling.

In Desi Evans' interviews, we find the mothering discourse producing accounts of sequences of action that are characteristic of the middle class. She is a full-time housewife; her husband is a professional (a secondary school teacher) and they have two children—one in junior Kindergarten (age 4) and one in grade 1 (age 6). She has read much of the popular literature on child rearing. When her daughter was small, a neighbor, a Montessori teacher, brought Desi a number of child-rearing books to read. She told us that she attended to the advice columns and articles in the newspaper and women's magazines, though with less interest than when her children were smaller. She has enrolled her son in several classes at the community center as a way of teaching him skills that would not be available at the school and as a way of preparing him for his school experience. She participates actively in the mothering discourse and orients her child-rearing practices to what she learned.

Anne Dexter lives in a working-class neighborhood with her husband, a driver for the city's mobile library, and their four sons whose ages range from 6 months to 10 years. She too is a full-time housewife. She volunteers one morning per week at the school library. In the past, she told us, she had been interested in reading about child rearing or watching programs on the topic on the TV, but no longer has this interest. She does not have time, and after four children, she "sort of knew what [she] was doing."

These two women described their mothering work very differently. Desi Evans talked about her activities and family interactions in terms that oriented us to the child development discourse. She organized her mothering for schooling based, in large part, on a knowledge of children that was congruent with the mothering discourse, as well as on her own preferences for her children's development. She was concerned about maximizing her children's potential for learning and development in all aspects of their lives. She herself is particularly interested in music, so this is a significant part of the supplementary educational work that she does with her children. Her approach is planned. She takes her son to various activities during the afternoons—a craft program, a gym and swim program, and so on. Next year, she plans to take him to a preschool program in which children are taught music through the use of cymbals, drums, and other percussion instruments. Her daughter takes piano lessons at school during her lunch hour and will move to private lessons in the next year. Ms. Evans' enjoyment of music is one impetus for involving her children in music. Another stimulus is her concern to maximize her children's potential for learning and development in all aspects of their lives.

In contrast, Anne Dexter seldom referred to her or her husband's role in developing her children. Rather she talked about their individual personalities and how that shaped their school experiences, or she had criticisms of the children's teachers. One son was having serious difficulties in grade 3 (age 8) that she attributes to his shyness: "And I said [to the teacher], really, he is very shy. Not shy as much as just quiet, and it takes him usually a few months or so to get used to the kids and the teacher every year. So I said: I expect his report will be much better, but we'll see." In telling us about these difficulties, Anne gave no excuses, no indication of self-blame. Shyness was represented as just a given of her son's personality and a family trait. She did not give any indication of being familiar with a child development discourse that might have suggested that shyness is a result of child rearing inadequacies of some kind. Nor did she represent her son's shy behavior in school as something that might be changed. Rather it was a character trait to be accepted and adapted to. She was, however, highly critical of the teacher whom she described as "horrible."

These differences between Dexter and Evans are generated, we suggest, by a difference in their participation in the mothering discourse. Desi Evans is right in there; what she had to say is organized by its conventions and knowledge resources. Anne Dexter, on the other hand, locates herself differently so that her son's problems do not appear to her as matters for which she is somehow responsible. She cares for him and is concerned with seeing that he gets treated properly at school, but there is nothing in what she says that might indicate in any way that she feels responsible for her son's shy behavior in school.

It is impossible, of course, in social research to escape the historically given culture of which the researchers are part. Indeed, we have clearly been exploring it as insiders. We were lucky to have discovered at least some of our presuppositions in the course of our study. We've come to the view that at least part of the power of a feminist ethnographic approach in sociology comes from the freedom to learn in the course of doing the ethnography, as well as in the work of reflection and analysis. Our ethnographic focus on learning from women, as much as we could, about the actual work they were doing in relation to their children's schooling means that however the story-building process was organized by the mothering discourse, it could not obscure the ordinary everyday realities of the work to which they were committed and which they could talk about. We have relied on these accounts in the chapters that follow.

3

TIME, SCHEDULING, AND COORDINATING THE UNCOORDINATED

In this and the following chapters, we explore the social relations organizing the work that women do in relation to their children's schooling and the work of the school. Out of the many topics we could have addressed, we have taken up two, both of which locate aspects of the work done in the home that are distinctively consequential for the work of schools. In this chapter, we look at how women coordinate the everyday scheduling disjuncture between paid employment, both theirs and their husbands, and the scheduling of the school. We draw on our interviews at both Turner's Crossing and Maltby. Our Turner's Crossing interviews gave us a greater richness of data largely because our interviewing time was not constrained. When we had to shift our research to Maltby, we had to deploy a more economical style of interviewing in order to get the research completed during the funding period. Hence, we have used more of our Turner's Crossing material in this chapter.

As we noted in the Introduction, we interviewed mothers in two neighborhoods in Turner's Crossing and two in Maltby. In Maltby, we also interviewed educators from two local schools—Uptown and Downtown—as well as central office administrators. As we worked on and thought about our material, we came to focus increasingly on time as central to the social relations that organize inequalities of class through schooling. Time here is not considered an abstract property, but rather as "the time it takes." It is a dimension central to our generous conception of *work*. There is no recognizable economy of women's time as mothers. It has no monetary value and is not recognized as taking time. The mothering discourse explored in the last chapter presupposes that mothers' time is indefinitely expandable and expendable. Hence, not having time is no excuse for failures to meet its expectations.

The family household as a work organization is structured by the schedules of organizations external to it —the scheduling of the shift or working day, the schedule of school, the opening hours of stores, the scheduling of leisure activities, vacations, and the major holidays. Daily household routines, however, are organized around the diverging schedules of family members' paid work or school schedules. School schedules and paid work schedules are not coordinated. The scheduling of paid work is designed in terms of the requirements of the employing organization. Shift work is fitted to maximize the use of equipment and plant. The work of salaried employees is in many instances organized around the ongoing requirements of what has to get done without attention to hours of work. The prescribed boundaries of the employed working day are set by requirements such as these, and not by the schedules of family members. There certainly are instances where employers have been interested in employing married women and have specifically adjusted the employed working day to the schedules of school and their husband's work. Paula Jackson (Maltby, Downtown School) is the only one among those we talked to whose work hours were adapted to her daughter's school schedule and her husband's shifts. For the most part, the design of school or work schedules does not take other schedules into account. The scheduling of the start of the school day, the timing of lunch, and the end of the school day is not adapted to the paid work schedules of family members. In this sense, these various schedules are externally uncoordinated—a problem that may be compounded where there are children of different ages living in the same household. A vivid picture of the ways in which the demands of different schedules may conflict is given by Alison Lawrence in her story of a "bad mothering moment" published in *The Globe and Mail*, a Canadian newspaper:

> When my daughter went to the school up the street, many mornings we would scream up to the school as the bell was ringing, and I would throw her knapsack after her and yell "Run! Run!" At one point in my career, I was working about an hour's commute from Toronto and would leave work at 11 p.m., driving hell-bent-for-leather down Highway 400 to pay off the babysitter and collapse into bed, and my daughter would climb in with me at 8:15 the next morning. But we would still get to school for that 8:55 bell. (Lawrence, 2002, p. A24)

We would guess that Alison Lawrence is a single parent. Her story illustrates the kinds of coordination problems that the workplace and school schedules impose on the daily order of the household. In what follows, we display, from the mother's side, the daily work of producing the routine schedule of the school day under conditions that don't always make it easy.

In all our interviews, it is the responsibility of the housewife and mother to coordinate family schedules, both taking direct responsibility for others and in how she coordinates the other functions of the family household into a daily routine, for example, the provision of meals. Schedules are not automatic. Schedule regularities, such as the beginning and ending of the school day are produced (and sometimes fail to be produced) primarily through the work of mothers.

CONSTRUCTING THE SCHOOL DAY

To appreciate the extent of the structured relationship between the family and the school, the compulsory character of the schooling process must be pictured. In Ontario, children between the ages of 6 and 16 must attend school every weekday. Attendance is legally enforceable by the truant officers, the courts, children's services, and so forth. As well, the child's attendance at school is required in order to maintain family welfare benefits. Schools keep records of children's attendance and check with the home if a child is not present and there is no note from a parent giving a reason for her or his absence.

A family household's daily routines are linked intimately to the school schedule over a period of more than nine years for each child. Organizing children's relationship to the scheduling of school and paid work is itself work. The basic schedules of individual family members that are coordinated in the home are inflexible—school is compulsory; employment is a necessity. Schedules are usually not coordinated and each represents a constraint on how meals are scheduled, how the supervision of children is provided for, when other household tasks are performed and shopping done, when time is available for doing the pedagogical work associated particularly with the first few years of schooling, and so on. This is almost exclusively women's work, or at least women's responsibility.

The School Day: Getting There on Time

The regularity of the school day is not produced entirely in the school nor is its production located in any one household's routines. Rather, it is produced for a school by the degree to which parents in a given area can consistently sustain the regularity of the school day against competing demands. Whether in paid work outside the home or not, organizing the household around the school day confronts mothers with varying difficulties. We met Anne Dexter in the previous chapter. She has four children ranging in age from 14 months to 10 years and doesn't work outside the home. She described her household's first-thing-in-the-morning routine:

> Oh well, the alarm usually goes off at 7:30. After I push the snooze button a couple of times, we're usually up by quarter to eight . . . [She begins to tell us that she gets the children up next but continues] No, normally I don't yell at the kids because they're usually up already. They're either playing in the room or watching TV, so, and they're mostly dressed by that time, too. They usually get dressed before they come downstairs (with the exception of the youngest).

Getting breakfast and getting them "out of the door" is a bit tumultuous and getting the timing right is both precarious and important:

> From 8:30 to 8:45 I'm yelling at them. Well, David's really the only one. He's got lace-up boots and it takes him—it seems it takes him 15 minutes to do these laces up. Well, he has to have them tight! Well, you're not going to lose them! He's sitting there going "Uuaarrgh!" I'm surprised the laces haven't broken, but maybe that's what he's hoping for. But the others just have pull-on boots so they're dressed and gone in a minute. But him! I start at 8:30. I should—I was thinking of getting a timer. Just saying "Listen, this is the time. When this bell goes off you've got no more time!" Except that I've priced timers and they're ten dollars! I'll keep yelling for a while!

Joanne Couzyn's only son is 6. She is manager of a restaurant and does not have to leave for work until after her son has left for school. She plays a more active part than Anne does but her son Jimmy also plays his part:

> I wake Jimmy up about 7:45 and ask him if he would like his breakfast and normally he says no, he doesn't want anything to eat. So I make sure that hands, face are washed, teeth brushed, lay his clothes out for him to get dressed, he gets dressed, makes his lunch for school ('cause he's in a lunch program, because I'm unable—

the only day I'm home is Thursday) and he usually watches the TV before he goes to school. He leaves for school at 8:30.

Older children take more of the responsibility. Astrid Baker works full time as a retail clerk. Her children, both girls, are 12 and 10. They get themselves up in the morning:

> And it's 7:30 when the kids get up. Half the time I have to wake them up, most of the time they get up on their own before 7:30. They come down, they get breakfast: cereal, toast, you know, that sort of thing.

Some husbands get themselves up in the morning and off to work without their wives' help, but some do not. Joanne Couzyn tells us, "My husband gets up for work about 6 . . . and he's gone by the time I get up." But Astrid Baker is more actively involved in getting her husband off to work: "Well the alarm goes off at 6. I usually crawl out at anywhere from 6:45 to 6:50, get him off to work, usually he has a glass of milk, some toast, and he's off to work." Though husbands may play a part in seeing the children out of the door, none of the husbands of the women we talked to were involved in the preschool routine of shepherding the children through the necessary preparations to be on time for school. It was the mothers who organized breakfast and coordinated dressing, except where children were old enough to take care of these tasks themselves.

We met Desi Evans in the previous chapter also. She does not work outside the home. Her husband is a professional with an adequate family income. She has organized a car pool so that most days her children are picked up in the morning and at noon; her daughter is returned to school after lunch and back home at the end of the school day. But Desi Evans's scheduling is quite complicated because her two children go to different schools and the schools have different timetables: Her daughter is in grade 1 and begins school at 9:00 a.m. Her lunchtime begins at 11:45 and continues until 1:00. School is finished for the day at 3:45. Her son, on the other hand, begins junior kindergarten at 9:30 and is finished at 11:15. She is in a carpool for both children. Making it all work is far from easy. The woman driving the carpool on any particular day must get one group of children to school before 9:00 a.m. while the other children do not have to be there for another half an hour. Then, at lunchtime, one child must be picked up at 11:15 while the other is not ready to come home for lunch until 11:45. The necessity for car pooling, particularly in the harsh Ontario winter, means that Desi Evans must bring games or books for reading in order to keep the children and herself entertained within the confines of a family car. There is no waiting room at the school and the amount of time that she can spend in the school with her carpool children is limited. As she says:

> Some things take so much time. The days I'm on the go, back and forth to school, it's a lot of time and a lot of responsibility. Driving the children to the school, unloading at the school, making sure they get into the classroom . . . . It's a lot of running around, a lot of hassle.

Other mothers walk their younger children to school. The moment when her child was able to take responsibility for getting there herself was, for Margaret Cartwright, a significant relief from an onerous, all-weather chore:

> Interviewer: How do the children get to school? How does Becky get to school?
>
> Margaret: This year, she goes on her own. Last year, for part of the year, I walked her. There is a crossing guard but it is a bit busy —midtown. Because she had not gone on her own and crossed the streets, I walked her part of the way. But now I had to—half way through the year, it was too much. Joel was, well now he is a boy but he was like a baby last fall . . . . It was a bit hard always going out. So finally somebody had to say that the best thing to do is you have to break that half way through. I slowly watched her and I noticed that she was excellent. She looked both ways, I mean a bit too much at first. She'd be standing there. She could have gone so many times, cross the street if I was with her and she's still the same. You know, you're with them; they don't look, even if you say so. But when we would both, more or less took turns because Ellis [her husband] was here at lunch and that. And if we stood back and she didn't even know we were there and we just watched her, she was excellent in getting across. But if she knew that you were there or even ten feet away, somehow she knew and she wasn't as aware and didn't really look out for herself.

Some children want more independence:

> M: I usually drive him to school. It's not that far but considering the health he's been in this past winter, I usually get up and run

him over to the school. But in the fall and that I did the first week and then there is a young lad next door who is in grade 7 or 8, he used to come over and get Anthony and walk him to and from school because it was getting time where Tony was saying "I want to go by myself. I don't want mommy taking me anymore." And then when winter started, he was becoming sicker and he was away from school 7 weeks out of the past winter. Then I just get up and drive him now till the warm weather comes and then he will start to walk again with the young lad next door.

A number of the women we talked to had paid employment and found themselves under scheduling pressures of various kinds. Some had schedules that were relatively easily combined with the morning organization of getting children off to school. Some mothers found ways of combining the increasing responsibility that older children were able to assume with ingenious forms of supervision with older children taking on more responsibility for the school day. Astrid leaves for work as a retail clerk before her children leave for school. They take responsibility for getting themselves ready for school and for leaving to be there on time. She has established a system of supervision by telephone. Before they leave for school they telephone her at work so that she can check up on their preparations:

> Before they go to school they phone me . . . and you know it's basically a run down of, you know, "have you got your books with you?" and with Blaine, "have you got your glasses?" because, I guess I shouldn't say she doesn't like wearing them, but she neglects to wear them an awful lot. "What coat are you wearing? You should wear your heavy coat, 'cause it's cold." You know.

Others with younger children find the rigors of paid work and school schedules difficult and stressful. Janie Apple's experience is perhaps an extreme, but it forcibly illustrates the kinds of problems that can arise. She works part time as a nurse in a hospital near her home. She works shifts, although the majority of them are graveyard shifts since the full time nurses have been able to organize their schedules to include fewer night shifts. When Janie works the 11 p.m. to 7 a.m. shift, she returns home by 7:20, gets to bed by 8:00 and is up again by 12:00 p.m. when her daughter may come home from school for lunch. When she is on day shift, she starts work at 7:00 a.m. and must leave home by 6:40. Her husband starts work at 6:45 a.m. and must leave home by 6:00 to reach work on time. So when Janie works either graveyard shift or day shift, she must have a baby-sitter come in at 6:00 a.m. and stay until noon. The combination of shift work and the early starting hours of her husband have combined to make the management of her children's supervision difficult. When the requirements of the school's starting time is added to the scheduling of her work and the difficulties of finding a baby-sitter, the mothering work routines become very complicated and difficult to maintain. As she described them here:

> Well, now that I have a baby-sitter come to the house, I always get the clothes (for the next day's school) out for the both of them. I leave them on the kitchen table and she takes care of Adrianne and . . . but they don't like her right now so I've done everything the same as if I wasn't working. I come home and I've given them breakfast and I've dressed them and I've combed their hair because they're not taking to her at all. But I haven't worked a day shift yet that she's had to baby-sit. But if I did, she would have to dress them and all what I do.

As she notes, day care for her children is not an option. Day care centers have schedules that are not coordinated with the shift work hours she has to maintain. She's low in the seniority rankings at the hospital so she doesn't get to choose which shifts she will work. Some weeks she has to start her shift before her school-age daughter's school day begins and has to take her and the younger child over to a baby-sitter before going to work. Thus, her management of her daughter's schooling schedules involves endless difficulties in finding baby-sitters to bridge the gaps in supervision created by the lack of coordination among the three individual schedules—her husband's, her own, and her elder daughter's.

Alice Orton, whose eldest son attends the Uptown School in Maltby, is in a similarly tight situation in the squeeze between the schedules of school and her paid work.

> I: So let's go through the kind of day that you have . . . For example, what do the kids do during the day; one is in school and one is in . . . ?
> Alice: One goes to a girlfriend, it's a private day care . . . she's in (the neighbouring small town) but she's had Matthew since he was 6 months old so I hate to change him. He needs some stability.[1]
> I: So you get the kids ready and then you take him to the neighbouring small town.
> A: On the way to work, yes.
> I: And if you have to go early, how does Matthew . . . ?

A: Well, my baby-sitter in Maltby, like I have a baby-sitter in Maltby, a neighbor, who takes him before and after school. And she's really flexible as to when he can be there . . . . It started out when I moved to Maltby a year ago. I was looking for a baby-sitter for him and my immediate next-door neighbor said she would do it. Then come Christmas, she went back to work so I was looking again. So I put an ad in the Maltby newspaper and had no response to it and I was getting really kind of panicky—I was off over Christmas for a couple of weeks so . . . . And then I happened to notice an ad—I was looking in the newspaper and I noticed an ad from somebody looking for baby-sitting and I called her and it turned out to be a neighbor two doors down that had just moved in November. And so it worked out really well . . . .

I: What time do you leave in the morning?

A: I leave somewhere between 6:30 and 7:00 most mornings. So he's usually there between 6:45 and 7:00 . . . [and he comes] back from school to her.

I: And what time do you get home?

A: I get home about 6:30 to 6:45 at night.

I: So you're gone for about 12 hours.

A: Yes . . . . It is a long day at times. It is for the kids too because they're usually up around 6 so . . . .

I: So do you give the kids breakfast and all that stuff before they go?

A: I do, yes.

I: And what about clothes and that kind of thing. Do you set it all out the night before, or how do you manage that?

A: Usually I try to set it out—I have in my head what I want them to wear the night before, and then it's just a matter of putting it on their bed when I get up in the morning. That's what I generally do . . . .

I: So do you find that's quite difficult to keep that all organized?

A: It is at times. You find it's hard to coordinate—especially if my schedule isn't flexible, like one day when I'm not going to be going into the office until a little later on, or something. I find that—oh, gee, did I let the baby-sitter know I'm not coming and things like that. I find it's a little hectic having the boys in two different locations, and like that. There are problems that you wouldn't have if they were both going to the same baby-sitter. Because it means communicating everything twice, even just things like: their grandfather's going to pick them up; they've got a doctor appointment, and stuff like that.

Astrid Baker's two daughters, 11 and 12 years old, have taken on a good deal of responsibility for themselves, supplemented by the support of Astrid's mother who lives next door and by Astrid's use of the telephone to supervise. Astrid leaves for work before her children leave for school and they take responsibility for getting themselves ready for school and for leaving to be there on time. Before they leave for school they telephone her at work so that she can check up on their preparations (as quoted above). In her accounts, we can see the thinking, commitment, and effort that goes into producing the normality of the school day, and the special stresses involved in producing that normality when mothers are in full-time paid work.

The kind of commitment involved became more evident in talking to the one or two women who did not share it. The difference might be described as one between homes that are dedicated to their children's schooling as a central project of their organization and those in which other objectives, such as the economic well being of the family, take precedence. This does not mean that parents are uncaring or uninterested in their children's education. It does mean that their paid work routines are the focus of the organization of their time.

Carol Irwin has taken on the responsibility of doing deliveries as a way of supplementing the family income. Sometimes she is out into the early hours of the morning and finds it difficult to get up in time to get her daughter Jasmine off to school in time. Here is her account:

> Carol: Well I have to . . . she gets up normally, this is quote normal unquote. I'll call her and I'll come downstairs and I'll make the coffee . . . . She will fiddle around up there. And I have to yell, you know, "Jazz! Get ready. Come on . . . ." She's not a great breakfast eater in the morning. I try to get toast or something down her in the morning. She likes grapefruit. A lot of the time I will make her egg and [indistinct] . . . .
> I: Does David [her husband] get his own breakfast?
> C: . . . she is not a real egg eater, either—just real, real soft eggs she'll eat. Won't eat fried or anything like that and . . . she'll [indistinct] up there and I'll get her down here, finally.
> I: Uh, huh. What time does she have to get off to school?
> C: 8:30 . . . .
> I: 8:30, and does she get herself—
> C: . . . she's got to be at Dorie's . . . .
> I: —going or do you get her going?
> C: Oh, yeah, she's not bad 'cept from watching the TV. Because it got so that she got up in the morning—if I sleep in and she was watching TV—she won't wake me.

I: . . . so she would just leave it go, as it was . . . ?
C: Yah. If I overslept, she wouldn't get herself off to school; she would come in and wake me up. At least the first few times, I can say, where she would try that. I would say to her, you know "you have a responsibility too, not to me but to yourself—that you go to school."

On both visits to Carol's home, Jasmine, her daughter was at home apparently for no particular reason.

The School Day: Lunch Time

At the time of our original study, in the mid 1980s, Ontario elementary schools were required to have a lunch program. Children were provided with a room in which to eat their lunches and were supervised by either school staff or parent volunteers. However, in all the descriptions of those programs by both parents and school staff, it was very clear that the children of the women we interviewed rarely stayed at school over the lunch period. One principal described how he tries to encourage children to go home at lunchtime unless there is no supervision in the home—that is, if the mother and father are both at work. Consequently, the timing of the school lunch period structures the mother's schedule in very direct ways. Lunch time includes the prior preparation of lunches for those children who stay at school, the organization of the mother's work day in order to ensure supervision and lunch for her children in the home, and the strategic use of other family members, neighbors, or baby-sitters to manage the gaps in childcare that arise in the conflicting demands of school, household, and labor market.

Lunch hour timing is quite tight. Anne Dexter says that she should get her sons to brush their teeth before they leave for school after lunch but it's a squeeze.

The only problem is at lunchtime. They're only home for such a short time that if they, by the time you think about getting them to brush their teeth it's time to go to school, and all three of them in the bathroom at the same time is just . . . not worth the aggravation, so normally I'll give them an apple.

They only have about forty minutes for lunch and Anne is as tuned in to the start of the school's afternoon program as she is for the beginning of the school day. "They get out at 11:45, but they normally get home about 12:10, especially in the snow. And they have to be back, the first bell goes off at 1:05."

The lunch period finds women who are in paid employment relying on a variety of supports. Janie Apple described her various strategies for organizing the lunch hour depending on whether she is working days, afternoons or graveyard shift. "The days that I'm working, she takes her lunch. And the days that I'm off, I leave it strictly up to her. I say to her if she wants to walk home, she only gets to spend like 30 to 35 minutes so it's not very long." Janie would prefer her daughter to come home for lunch because "They can't buy anything at school to drink or anything." And,

> She likes to come home better than stay at school. And they en-
> courage the children to be coming home for lunch because, well,
> they say it gives them a nice break from being in the environment
> of school. And also, they get hot lunches at home which. . . . So I
> leave it up to her, I ask her the night before if she wants to come
> home and it's usually she does want to come home on the days
> that I'm off. In fact, even some days, like when I'm on night shift
> I'm usually up by noon hour and she'll want to come home but
> I usually encourage her to stay at school those days because you
> never know, I may sleep in longer and the baby-sitter—and I'm
> only paying her to look after one child so. . . .

In the Dexter household, both parents take responsibility for being at home and making lunch for the children. Generally it is Anne who is there to make the children's lunch but sometimes her husband takes over. When neither parent can be at home, the children still come home to pick up the lunch pail that Anne has prepared for them and go to eat lunch at the home of the woman who baby-sits the Dexter's 14 month old son.

Astrid Baker's mother "lives right next door" and the children often eat their lunch there. When their grandmother is not at home, her two daughters are now able to get their own lunch with their mother's tele-phone supervision.

> When my mother's not home, they come home and they make
> their own lunch. Cassie's just started this year, you know, to make
> a bowl of some soup. She'll phone me and say "I want soup for
> lunch." and I'll say "Okay, well what are you going to do?" Like
> they'll phone me at lunchtime when they get home from school.
> "What are you having for lunch" you know. If they want a sand-
> wich, peanut butter goes quite well. If the day is cold and they
> want soup, then I'll ask her what she's going to do, how she's

going to make it. She tells me. I say, "Fine, after you've made it phone me." Which she does.

Barbara Lindsay, whose son has been ill recently, picks him up from school for lunch and takes him back again for the beginning of afternoon school. Alice Orton, who works full time, makes lunches for both her children the night before. "I hate making lunches so I have to do it; I force myself no matter what time it is, before I go to bed to do the lunches."

The School Day: Coming Home

The daily household routine must provide for continuous supervision of children when they are not at school. The daily schedule must take into account when the children will be returning from school, ensuring that there will be an adult at home or that they have another home to go to in which there will be a responsible adult. Janie Apple's husband returns home from work before her daughter gets home and this introduces some flexibility into Janie's routines. When she is not working dayshift, she may go shopping in the afternoon—not grocery shopping but, as she says, "shopping shopping" in the downtown area. She takes her younger daughter with her. She remarks, as if rationalizing her absence, that her husband does not have anything to do because her older daughter likes to sit and watch television for an hour when she gets home. Joanne Couzyn, on the other hand, is never home when her son comes back from school. Her work hours begin in late morning or early afternoon, and for four days of the week she does not return until it is nearly suppertime. After school, her son goes to her sister-in-law's house. She lives just round the corner and her son goes to the same school, so the two boys walk home together. At other times, and for other mothers, discrepancies between the mother's employed work schedule and her children's school schedule are filled in by the husband, by neighbors, or by family living nearby.[2]

Our interviews gave us a picture of how women as mothers of primary school children organize their work to produce the regularity of the school day. For those such as Alice Orton who have full-time jobs, management of the conflicting schedules calls for thought and organization. Rather than viewing the school day as an institutional given, we can see some of the mothering work that goes into its production.

The School Day at School

Talking to teachers at Uptown and Downtown Schools in Maltby we learned something of the significance of mother's contribution to the production of the school day at school for teachers' work, and how they adapt to situations where they cannot take for granted that all the members of the class will regularly be present on time.

The scheduling of the day's work in school relies on children coming to school on time. The curriculum is organized for group teaching in either small or large groupings. The work of teaching is increased each time a lesson must be repeated for a child who has not been present in the class during the lesson. Teachers told us of the importance of curricular scheduling. In Uptown School, teachers could rely on children being in their desks and ready to start their schoolwork when the morning bell rang. In Downtown School, however, teachers could not make that assumption. Most children were on time for school in the morning, but enough of them were late that the teachers' schedules had to be changed to accommodate the latecomers. In this section, we explore the school day at school and note the differences between the two schools. As we will see, the school day, while fixed in policy, is often variable in practice. These differences have consequences for the time the teacher has for teaching and for the learning time available to the students.

At Uptown School, the school day almost always starts and ends at the scheduled times. Here's an Uptown teacher's response to a question about the school schedule and attendance:

> Teacher: Well for me, my timetable is my lifeline. I couldn't survive without it. Like you said, you have so many things to juggle that you just have to stick to it. Even if you're sick a day it throws you off for a week. You know, and you just dread being away for a day.
> I: So is that something that is important to you in terms of the children . . . their being on time?
> T: Oh yes. And I have never had any problems in this class with kids being late. I, sometimes, in other years, have had problems and I've had to speak to parents and let them know that time is very important and the kids have to be prompt and they can't miss days. They can't afford to miss days, this type of thing.

At Uptown, the curriculum is mapped onto a schedule in which time per subject is allocated by numbers of minutes. The vice principal of Uptown School described the increasingly regulated organization of curriculum delivery.

> I: So the setting of curriculum goals is also part of how you coordinate the relation between different classrooms to different resources, and over time and . . . .

Vice Principal: That's right. The other thing that's checked, of course, is that they're offering enough time for each subject. We have time goals there behind you on the board [directing the interviewer's attention to a complex timetable on the board behind her] . . . . The second one from the corner at the top—the number of minutes per week per subject is very clearly set out and that's checked. It's not a hard and fast rule where it's one or the other.

I: So you have to work within those time frames.

VP: That's right. And this is the week we're doing all this . . . . The principal and I, this morning, just went over each teacher's timetable for the 6-day cycle. What we looked for this morning specifically was, and this is another initiative from above kind of thing, are the teachers blocking large blocks of time for language arts rather than saying "Well, I've got a half hour spelling program over here each day and I've got writing down here because it just happens to fill up the last 20 minutes and somebody else is doing my grammar because I trade off for gym." And that's not acceptable any more. Teachers are being directed that language arts is being handled now by one teacher in large blocks and integrated with the rest of the day as much as possible in terms of subject matter and in terms of activity centers and so on.

The possibility of delivering such a precisely calculated allocation of time to curriculum subject relies on children's punctuality. Uptown School was clearly able to take this for granted in a way Downtown School was not.

At Downtown School, late arrivals were normal. We don't mean by this that many children were late in arriving or even that it was a regular occurrence. On the other hand, both teachers and principal, in response to our question on the topic, stated that arriving late was something that could be expected and that they were prepared for. The principal described his energetic attempts to change the ways of particular students who were regularly arriving late. He saw the problem both in terms of educational loss to the individual and as introducing problems into the classroom:

Principal: If they are not there ready to go when the bell goes, then they are behind the eight ball before the day even starts. You don't know what the teacher was doing. You walk into the middle of the lesson and they cannot catch up if the teacher has already spent time to introduce the lesson properly, they can't redo it and take that time and give the basic reason for it and the fundamentals. Okay, whatever lesson it is. [R: Yes.] That means the child has to be there to get the full benefit of it. Sure the teacher can go with him and tell him in three minutes what to do, but the child has missed all the examples et cetera, that go with it. So for the child's own sake it's important. Besides that, they come in and become a focal point for the rest of the children. So we have this social problem starting to crop up. Either he becomes the center of attraction or he feels badly that everybody is looking at him and that he is late. The other side of the picture is what's it doing to the class? When he comes in late the teacher has to swipe all the time from every other student to get that child up to where they are and then get that child working.

A Downtown grade 1 teacher had clearly adapted the morning routines so that late arrivals would be minimally disruptive.

I: What effect does it [a child being late] have on your work?
T: Well we have morning exercises from the office through the PA, and so therefore they miss that and then they usually get there. There aren't that many that are that late. That's the program. And then, if they go from that to writing their morning log which is an individual thing and so maybe they will miss writing their log that morning or something other like that. But usually there isn't anybody coming in really late—that comes in the middle of a reading program or anything like that because these introductory things take until 9:30. But I really get on them it they are late two or three times.

In contrast to the Uptown School teacher, the Downtown teacher's school day routine begins with rather flexible activities that don't require the children to share a common curricular focus.

The tight school scheduling in Uptown relies on the work done by women at home, and the more permeable time boundary of the start of the Downtown School day indicates a neighborhood in which household commitment to sustaining the school schedule is less consistent.

CONCLUSION

It is here that we can begin distinguishing between the home that has the social and economic resources and is dedicated to maintaining the project of the children's successful schooling, and the home that, for whatever reason, does not or cannot place that project at the center of its scheduling of the work day. In this chapter, our emphasis has been on how a variety of family situations produces, or fails to produce, the standardized order of the school day. Perhaps there are several children. Perhaps the child is ill for a period of weeks. Maybe part-time work hours can be adjusted to the exigencies of the school day. Where mothers are working full-time, or are on shift work, they have to exercise considerable ingenuity, have some luck in finding childcare, and be capable of sustaining a consistent and often arduous commitment to fitting together complex schedules. At the time of our study, Downtown School was allowing students to come a half hour earlier, which must have been helpful to some, though it did not solve Carol Irwin's problem of her late night work schedule and disposition to sleep late in the morning. None of the schools provided extended after-school childcare. Some schools, particularly in Turner's Crossing, discouraged children staying in school to eat lunch.

On the one hand, the school imposes its order on the routines of the household, just as does the scheduling of paid work. On the other, the school relies on the work and commitment of (primarily) women to sustain that order as a local practice. However, it is a local practice that is always at risk. In some neighborhoods, such as that of Downtown School, the school day was always being reasserted. Teachers gave children detentions for being late. The principal spoke to parents about their children's attendance. Carol Irwin cautioned her daughter not to answer the phone when the family had slept in. The principal bought alarm clocks for some of the older students. In other neighborhoods, such as Uptown School, the school day has a taken-for-granted character. Students rarely missed lessons and teaching time could match the schedules set up by the principal and vice principal. Simply in terms of time on task, the students at Uptown School are receiving more instruction, and it is likely, scoring more highly on achievement tests than are students in Downtown School.

Getting children to school on time and being available when they come home from school, whether at lunch or after school, involves a coordinating of women's time. This may involve adjustments of various kinds when a woman is not in paid employment. If she has several children, that in itself, can create additional stresses on the work she has to do. Desi Evans' two children, for example, go to different schools. But the big problems come when a woman is in paid employment. Her schedule then is much less flexible. Downtown School allowed children to arrive at 8:30, and that flexibility was useful for those whose work started early. It didn't, however, work for Carol Irwin who worked late and was inclined to give sleep priority over getting her daughter to school in the mornings. Nor would it have worked for Janie Apple when she worked day shifts. The regularity of the school day was clearly supported in a school like Uptown School where the majority of families in the area conformed to the middle-class family model described in chapter 1. When this economically organized family condition was absent, the school day came into view as a process coordinated through the work of mothers and managed by educators.

4

COMPLEMENTARY EDUCATIONAL WORK

Studies such as those by Annette Lareau (1987) have emphasized the significance of parental involvement for giving an educational advantage to children in school. Her study finds that middle-class parents are active in their children's school and schooling. They monitor their children's progress in school to ensure that the kinds of educational opportunities needed are available to their children. Parents whose children attend a school with a population that is predominantly working class are not involved in the same way. Lareau's claim is that it is the difference in the parents' ability to fuse their children's cultural knowledge with that of the school that differentiates the educational outcomes for their children.

The approach we have adopted here stresses other aspects of schools and schooling. First, we focus less on the consequences for the individual child than on the part parents play in the work processes that go into the making of a school. A school is a complex of work processes; teachers, custodial staff, administrators, children, and parents are the main contributors to how a school operates. Their collective work is done within given administrative and budgetary contexts, within the constraints established by province or state and municipality and their fiscal practices. How schools can function is also constrained by the degree to which the curriculum is standardized, to the amount of standardized testing that is mandated, as well as by such other constraints as the teachers' associations or unions.

Our research and analysis focuses on the work of women who are mothers of elementary school children. In the previous chapter, we examined those aspects of parental work that contribute to the orderly scheduling of the school day. In this chapter, we explore their part in providing for their children, and hence to the school, educational work that complements the work children are doing in the school.

As we mentioned earlier, our research in Turner's Crossing was cut short before we could explore these topics systematically with those whom we interviewed. Because we are making comparisons in this chapter between parents with children in a middle-class and in a lower-income school, our discussion is restricted to those we talked to in Maltby whose children were attending either the Downtown or the Uptown School. In terms of occupation, the two groups of seven parents look like this:

Table 1 Parents' Occupations, Maltby Downtown School

Mother's occupation	Father's occupation
full-time secretary	shift work, Big Plant
housewife	civil engineer
housewife	shift work, Big Plant
full-time training	cab driver/odd jobs
full-time interviewing	shift work, Big Plant
housewife plus bookkeeping at home	shift work, Big Plant
various temporary jobs	shift work, Big Plant

Table 2 Parents' Occupations, Maltby Uptown School

Mother's occupation	Father's occupation
housewife	financial administrator
housewife plus lunch-hour supervisor at school, 5 hrs.	parts assembly
housewife	police
housewife plus 6 hrs part-time	general contractor
housewife	restaurant owner/manager
housewife plus 10 hrs part-time	assessor
full-time employed, customer service agent	
(single parent)	unemployed

As can be seen, there are substantial differences between the two groups. Only three of the women we talked to from the Downtown School district were full-time housewives. One was doing bookkeeping work at home, and four were involved full-time outside the home, though one of these was in training and another seemed to be involved virtually full-time in various temporary jobs in and outside the home. By contrast, the Uptown School parents look more like the middle-class family organization described in chapter 1. All but one of the men are involved in professional occupations or in business (restaurant owner and general contractor) and all but one of the women are full-time housewives, some of whom have short-hour part-time jobs on the side. The one woman who worked full-time was a single parent, largely responsible for the support of herself and her family because her husband was unemployed.

COMPLEMENTARY EDUCATIONAL WORK: A CONTRIBUTION TO THE SCHOOL

In this and the following two chapters we explore the work that parents do that complements the work done by teachers in school. In the first of these, we put forward the general formulation that guides our analysis, and we explore the accounts of mothers who are full-time housewives and the various ways they orient to and organize the educational work they do with their children (chapter 4). In the second of these chapters (chapter 5), we do the same for women who work outside the home. We also present what we learned about the contribution made by the children's fathers as well as summarizing what we have learned from these chapters.

The overall framework for our analysis follows Ann Manicom's thesis that the complementary educational work of parents makes a significant difference to the level at which a school can operate. Apart from whatever advantage parents' complementary work provides to the individual child, their work also contributes to the functioning of the school. This is the dimension of schools' functioning that our interviews with women with children in elementary school in Maltby enables us to explore. The level at which the required curriculum can be delivered varies with how much and what kind of educational work is delivered by parents. Communities in which the majority of parents are delivering considerable time and background knowledge to their children enable the school to operate at a higher overall level of achievement than those in which parents in general are able (for whatever reason) to provide only a moderate or low level of complementary educational work. Manicom's (1988) exploration of the ways in which teacher's work varies with the input of parents in a given community provides a telling account of the kinds of differences that emerge. Here, from her study, is a teacher from a school in a relatively affluent community describing the kind of difference it makes for the teacher's work when a child has had the experience of being read to at home:

The basic idea of knowing how to sit and listen to a story . . . .
You know if a child has never sat around and had an adult read
to them and they don't know how the pages work . . . . They're
things we just take for granted. Whereas a child who, from a very
early age, has been exposed to books . . . . Plus the patterning, the
predictability in a book, that the child knows what the next word
is going to be. Well, that helps.

Teacher A
Mixed/Affluent Neighborhood, Grade 2 (p. 180)

A teacher in an inner city school confirms this account of the basic
forms of competence that go into simply knowing how to listen to a
story being read:

Kids who come from an enriched background . . . have been exposed to language, language in all its many and varied forms.
Reading. They see the parents reading, they even see the eye
movements! . . . I mean, you don't think that the kids pick up
that, but they do. They are read to, they're asked questions, they
even know from the rising inflection that it's going to be a question. They have assimilated to some degree the strategies.

Teacher E
Inner city, grade 1 (p. 180)

Children from disadvantaged communities may not have acquired
some basic educational skills such as "holding the book properly, knowing it goes from left to right, knowing when a book is upside down. And
some of them don't have it. They're not used to being around books"
(Teacher D, Inner City, Primary, p. 178). Of course, these skills can be
learned in the school classroom. The problem is that if the teacher has
to give time to teaching them, she is giving less time to teaching the curriculum. As Manicom (1988) emphasizes, "a feature of being 'ready' for
reading includes skills that are not necessary for reading per se, but are
necessary for the teaching of literacy as it is organized in schools." (p.
182) Hugh Mehan (1979) has argued similarly that a child's participation in schooling depends on prior knowledge, such as knowing how to
take turns or to recognize that a question calls for an answer in a conversation, skills that are an essential part of a teacher's teaching reper-
toire. Schools in relatively affluent areas can count on parents who are
doing the background work that enables the school to meet curriculum
objectives. The inner city schools of the city in which Manicom's study

was done have difficulty. In inner city schools, the following situations are often the case:

> Teachers determine that they must spend more time on certain things, teaching children particular skills and habits before actually getting on with literacy. If children have trouble with scissors or glue, for example, or cannot work in groups at a listening station, the teaching of literacy is disrupted. Sometimes the disruption is a matter of the teacher constantly having to interrupt the group with which she is working in order to go to the aid of the others (which reduces the actual literacy teaching time for the group). Or she may devote considerable time in the first few months of school to develop readiness skills. She may abandon certain activities altogether. In these cases, she gets behind in covering her teaching tasks, where the normal pace has been defined by mandated curriculum materials and procedures[1] to accommodate the multiplicity of occurrences they experience. (Manicom, 1988, p. 183)

By *complementary educational work*, we mean work done by parents that contributes directly to a child's work as a learner in school. It includes the kinds of help parents in elementary school may give a child with her reading, with his spelling, with her math or with other specific skills that bear directly on the tasks a child is expected to do in school, including ensuring that any homework is done on time. Without discounting the significance of parental involvement in general, our interest in what parents contribute to their children's school is one of those aspects of their work that is directly complementary to the curricular, pedagogical, and administrative work of the school. The complementary educational work provided by parents in a given community creates the conditions under which the work of teaching is done. If teachers must spend time making up for what is absent from the preparation of at least some of the children in her class, then she or he has less time to spend on other educational objectives.

THE FULL-TIME HOUSEWIVES

In looking at some of the different ways in which the women we talked to were involved, or in at least a couple of instances, not involved, in educational work with their children, we have divided those we talked to in Maltby's Downtown and Uptown Schools into groups in terms of whether they worked outside the home or were full-time housewives.

We included in the category of full-time housewives those who worked less than 10 hours per week outside the home and the one woman who did bookkeeping at home. We also treated the full-time training program of one woman as the equivalent of a full-time job since it meant that she was not at home for that crucial after-school period. Nine of the women we talked to were full-time housewives, six of them with children in Uptown School and three in Downtown. The remaining five were employed or otherwise active full time outside the home.

The school day is a fixed feature of the weekday. Elementary school children come home in midafternoon. Some bring home what they've done at school to show their parents, some bring home tasks such as spelling to do at home, and some have homework. The time immediately after school is an important time when a parent can attend to school matters. Here is a key difference between the employed and the nonemployed women we talked to. Those who are full-time housewives are at home at crucial times of day. The times both before supper and after supper are at their disposal for taking up school matters with their child or children.

An adult being present when a child comes home from school means that the adult can look at what the child or children have brought home. There may be work done, a task assigned, or a note from the teacher. Reading or working with math can be built into the home routine of the afternoon. There is an opportunity for the parent to talk with the child about school, to respond to problems the child is experiencing, or to express interest and give praise. In our research, we discovered that what work was done and how varied greatly. Every family had its individual arrangements. In some families, the after-school educational work was highly routinized; in others, it fit more flexibly into other activities. Some outside activities were important components of the daily routine; others were not prominent. In our examination of the activities of parents with children that form part of the school day routine, we have grouped the accounts we received roughly in order of the extent to which the after-school day is dedicated to complementary educational work: skills specifically oriented to the school, such as reading, math, and spelling.

Table 3 Full-Time Housewives and Full-Time Employed Mothers, Uptown and Downtown Schools

	Uptown School	Downtown School
Full-time Housewife	Ames, Desmond, Fergus, Knight, Moore, Naysmith	Cartwright, Gordon, Lindsay
Employed	Orton	Ecker, Heller, Irwin, Jackson

We emphasize that in creating these groups, we did not evaluate the women we talked to as *mothers*. There are many ways of parenting, and different families embody different values in their practices. In many families, it was clear that school achievement was by no means the only value that guided parental activities with children. For some, sports such as soccer or swimming were also important, and in one or two of the interviews, other values appeared, such as what might be described as an orientation toward the inner life of the family. Our concern here is only with the extent to which parents' work contributes to their child's or children's educational achievement, and to which it can be seen as more or less directly complementary to the classroom, and hence, to the school's educational work.

We have drawn a simple division among the full-time housewives, between the highly routinized and the more flexible. It is not clear to us that this is a difference that arises from the amount of time and thought that goes into doing complementary educational work. The distinction, however, leaves room to show a range of choices for the ways mothering work is done—for example, choices such as a preference for allowing children time to play with friends or to engage in other activities versus time spent on activities of direct educational relevance. We do not mean in any way to be critical of mothers who view other activities as of equal or more importance than school-relevant work. We are concerned rather with what the complementary educational work parents contribute to the school and not with what they are contributing to the children.

Educational Work As a Priority

Martha Desmond's educational routines were the most thorough and complete. Her daughter Carol is in grade 1 and still comes home for lunch; her son Billy is in junior kindergarten. Martha and Carol scrutinize the work that Carol brings home from school together when Carol gets home both at lunchtime and after school:

> Well, Carol comes in at 4:00 and we do the same thing we do at noon. We go through her bag and she shows me all her stuff and if she has had trouble with something then we'll discuss it and she will go down and watch maybe a half an hour of television or she sits . . . sometimes she colors, sometimes she sits and cuts things out at the table while I get supper ready. We both have things to do. I set them up with little things to do.
>
> **Desmond**
> *Uptown, Maltby*

Martha and Carol do this together: "we" do the same thing as at lunchtime, "we" go through her bag. If a problem emerges when Martha goes over what Carol has brought home in her bag, it is dealt with right there and then. Schoolwork generates anxiety, as we find here and as we found with other women we talked to; there are problems to be dealt with—feelings that schoolwork has created for Carol:

> She's very conscientious, she'll bring a piece of work home and she thinks that everything should be correct all the time and I've been trying to tell her that it doesn't matter if you make a mistake. Next time you won't. That's how you learn. But if she's had trouble with it then I'll sit down and I'll go over it with her and the next day she knows that she knows it and then she's happy about it.
>
> **Desmond**
> *Uptown, Maltby*

We see here that Carol's troubles are school generated but not school governed. Carol comes home with her work marked as correct or incorrect by the teacher; these are not directions to her or her parents to take remedial action. But a less than completely correct performance troubles Carol. Martha takes this up in two ways: She helps Carol improve her capacity to perform at school—"I'll sit down and I'll go over it with her and the next day she knows that she knows it." She also tries to reorient Carol's response so that she doesn't get upset about mistakes.

Carol's after-school time is controlled and quite carefully managed. Martha and Carol have looked through the work Carol has brought home. Carol has half-an-hour or so to relax in which she "messes around in her room" or watches television. Then Martha sets up "little things for them [the two children] to do" and, while she prepares supper, Carol and Billy sit in the kitchen and do cut out, paste, and pencil play using books and toys that Martha has bought for that purpose. This enables Martha to supervise what they're doing:

> You kind of have to sit there. I do things in the kitchen and sort of supervise. They sit at the kitchen table and I might be making supper and they can do things like this or I could be making something for supper the next night or baking or anything and they'll sit and do that. We'll talk and things.
>
> **Desmond**
> *Uptown, Maltby*

Martha's organization of the day produces definite home time slots allocated to definite pieces of the overall enterprise. In the mornings after Carol has gone to school, she works with Billy who goes to school in the afternoons. After-school hours of both children are coordinated to make time for the school-relevant activities that Martha supervises. Martha leaves Carol's homework until after supper:

> I usually leave it. I let her have a snack at 4:00 and just leave it because she doesn't always feel like more schoolwork right after school so we just let it go.
>
> **Desmond**
> *Uptown, Maltby*

So the after-supper work period is given over to work directly governed by the school:

> We sit for about a half hour every night and read. Well she has her readers to go over and word lists that she has to know. So we sit and we go over the reading every night and over the words every night. The teacher sends a wordbook home. And it used to be like they got a new word everyday but now she sends a sheet of about thirty words a week which they have to know by the end of the week. They have a week and they have to know them. Now she must go over them with them [the children] at school but also you're to do it at home.
>
> **Desmond**
> *Uptown, Maltby*

Martha does more than listen to Carol read. She plays an active teacher-like role, putting work into developing games as exercises for Carol:

> Then she has readers that she reads to us and then if there's words that I know she doesn't know then I print out little sentences with the word in it and I have her underline the word so it kind of stays with her. And then if she is still having trouble then I make up little games where she cuts the words out and finds the words that match the word. So she learns to recognize it.
>
> **Desmond**
> *Uptown, Maltby*

Then there is "bedtime reading" and here Martha's husband Ray plays a role:[2]

> We have a bedtime story every night, one for each of them or maybe one together. It just depends on . . . if Ray is home he reads to Billy and I'll read to Carol or we'll switch. I'll take Billy and he'll take Carol. We read a story every night.
>
> **Desmond**
> *Uptown, Maltby*

The children's school day is carefully managed with educational objectives in mind. Martha's approach is strategic, taking into account her appraisal of the educational environment of her children, their personalities, and so forth. She works to bring the child's individuality into an effective relation with the institutional setting of the school. Thus she has decided to give Billy more direct preschool teaching than she had given to Carol. The strategic character of her thinking is apparent in the following discussion with the interviewer. She takes into account the level at which other kindergarten children are functioning, and the differing personalities of her two children, and incorporates what she has learned from her experience with Carol.

> Martha: I didn't do as much with her as I am with Billy.
> I: Why's that?
> M: Well, I find kids today are . . . they know a lot more before they start school. They just are smart to begin with . . . [and] I feel that Billy could use the extra . . . like I guess I didn't do it with her because she was outgoing and she has got a good bubbly personality and if she doesn't get the information she will get it, you know. She'll have her hand up and she'll ask questions and she questions everything. But Billy is shy and he's within himself a lot. And I thought well if I did more with him that when he came to kindergarten he's not going to stick and shake and he's not going to be like this. Then at least he'll know how to go about it. He won't be bewildered and upset inside over not doing it. So I thought we keep doing these little things and the teacher sets it out and gives him instructions and he doesn't quite catch it and he's afraid to ask, he'll know how to go about it.
>
> **Desmond**
> *Uptown, Maltby*

She has anticipated the kinds of projects Billy might have in the classroom and is trying to help him develop ways of acting that will be effective for him in the school setting. She has also learned from Carol's experience:

> She knew most of her alphabet and different things so I didn't go into her upper case and lower case. I didn't think it was any . . . and counting and all of that. But then when she hit kindergarten I realized well maybe I hadn't done enough.
>
> **Desmond**
> *Uptown, Maltby*

The kind of detailed attention Martha gives to her children's schooling, her scrutiny of their work, how they feel about it, and so forth, enables her to tune her practices to the individual and to modify them as circumstances or her knowledge of them change. Noteworthy is her concern with educating her children's attitudes towards school and schooling. She tries to teach Carol to treat her mistakes as experiences to learn from rather than to be upset about. Her preschool teaching of Billy is motivated, in part, by a concern with how his personality might be consequential for his school functioning. After-school time at the Desmond home is quite structured, and the children's activities are continually monitored and interpreted in relation to the educational project.

Amanda Knight's son, Richard, is still in kindergarten, and therefore she is not yet working with the same kind of pressure as will kick in when he reaches grade 1. Amanda, however, is like Martha in terms of the care with which the school day routines are designed with educational objectives in mind. As a conscious strategy, the home environment she creates for her three children (Richard is the oldest) is educationally saturated:

> Well I do the alphabet only because they want to. I have a little alphabet on the fridge or something and even David [the youngest child, scarcely more than a baby] who goes by, he wants me to tell him the alphabet. I find that kids are really interested in symbols at an early age. They want to learn it. If you put it handy where they can see it, they are interested. And not teaching that way only but you know, just going out in the garden and talking about it while you are doing it. Things like that where if they were looked after by somebody else who usually has their own kids

with them, they don't have time to sit down and say these little things, "this is a plant and this is a seed" or something like that. And I also take them to things like swimming during the day which they would have but I just think it's a little bit broader for them to see the world at an early age, opens more experiences to maybe want to learn in the future.

Knight
Uptown, Maltby

Her daughter, Stella, who is in preschool, isn't very interested at this time in learning math beyond numbering from one to ten, so Amanda makes math a part of the everyday environment by putting a math chart up on the refrigerator. Creating an educational environment responds to children's natural interest in symbols: "If you put it [symbols] handy where they can see it, they are interested." Her strategy is less one of direction than the education of children's own choices and energies through such means. Everyday activities, such as swimming, are seen as components of the educational project; swimming is more than fun, or healthful exercise, or the learning of a physical skill. While it may be any or all of these things, for Amanda it ties in to the educational project as "broadening children's experiences." Thought and planning are characteristic of Amanda's approach to mothering work:

There are even days when you, like now that I am starting to have more time, I finish my spring cleaning really early or something, I would say before I go to sleep, "Well, what will I do tomorrow with them?" Cause if you don't plan it you won't have time. Even if you're doing pasting and cutting, sometimes in the morning you'll get it ready cause if you say to them we're going to do pasting and cutting, right away they've gone on you and you have to run for the scissors. So it's better to have it all planned out what you are going to do. And often I think, well, if it's going to be a fun time or a learning time. Like sometimes I'll devote time to learning, just teaching them money or something like that. Or if grandma is gone to Acapulco we take the globe out and we see where it is and things like that.

Knight
Uptown, Maltby

Even in the kindergarten context, we find Amanda, like Martha Desmond, highly tuned to school standards and where her children stand in relation to them:

Richard is in kindergarten and every kid wrote a valentine to him and wrote their own name and his name. Every kid knows how to write. Every kid knows how to read a little bit. They know their colors and I think teachers are starting to assume this now. Cause I know when he writes something she is already saying "you should improve this writing" and things like this.

Knight
Uptown, Maltby

As with Martha, Amanda's experience of the standards of school performance, has led her to do more preschool teaching with her younger children. She tries to spend at least an hour per day doing educational work with both Stella and Richard:

At nursery school, they encourage them to put their own name on their work and I just think . . . . She is trying to you know, it starts usually when you write a birthday card to someone and say, "would you like to sign your name to grandma on this card?" and then they get interested in writing their own name. At least I find if you sort of encourage them that way, when they are about 3. So now she is interested in writing her name.

Knight
Uptown, Maltby

Here again we can see how Amanda enters everyday events into the educational project—a card to grandma becomes an occasion for interesting her daughter in learning to write her name. This everyday education is carefully planned.

The educational routines of the school day are tightly organized. Amanda doesn't ask Richard to do his homework as soon as he gets home. Instead, she prepares cut-and-paste play for the children at this time. Richard brings readers home from school to read from and memorize words, but Amanda does not believe in moving directly into schoolwork right after he gets home from school, nor in talking about school with him at that time. Later in the day, after supper, she goes over his work with him. Though Amanda and her children play games and fool around after supper as well, there is always reading also:

My kids have always. . . . I started reading them books since they were . . . just a picture book; you know, there's those big books with bold pictures. Even when they were about four months I'd lay on the floor with them and I would open them up and we would talk. Or I'd put it beside them. Like Richard, if he sees a book he'll come crying with it. And you can't just read one, you have to read ten of these little books. So we go to the library. They have tons of books of their own, but you get tired of the same ones. So I started reading to them early.

Knight
Uptown, Maltby

The daily household routines of Martha Desmond and Amanda Knight are tightly organized around the educational project. They plan, prepare, and supervise their children's activities in ways that are oriented to the acquisition of the kinds of skills that are specifically relevant to school. For the next group of mothers, school-oriented work is less focal in the organization of the school day. There is no less planning or involvement, but the orientation diversifies daily activities.

Diversified routines

Lisa Naysmith's (Uptown) husband, Stuart, works at Big Plant on day shifts in parts assembly. They have three boys: Art, who is 8 and in grade 3, Tim, 6 and in grade 1, and Jack, who is 5 and in kindergarten. The two older boys attend the same school and walk home together. Lisa keeps a close check on their arrival time. They should be home by 4:00 and if they are not she goes out to look for them. Mostly this is a problem in wintertime.

> I: Why would it happen then? Do they have school sports or something?
> Lisa: A lot of the sidewalks aren't cleared and it's really hard for the younger ones to trudge through the snow in the winter. There's also a hill that they like to slide down, snowball fighting. Then they come in and we usually try to do homework as soon as they come in.

Naysmith
Uptown, Maltby

It is important that they get home on time because they have a busy schedule. Homework must be done before dinner because, for much of the year, they are much involved in activities outside the home:

> L: We have Cubs and Beavers on Wednesday nights; in the summer time we have soccer four nights a week. We have skating les-

sons one night a week in the winter. In the fall and spring we have swimming lessons two nights a week.
I: So when do you get to stay home?
L: We don't.

Lisa takes up the teacher's recommendations in terms of what to focus on in working with Art and Tim. She has part-time employment at the school supervising the children's lunch, and this gives her opportunities for connecting with her children's teachers informally as well as in formalized meetings with them. Art, the oldest boy, has had problems learning to read, so Lisa has taken advantage of that experience to anticipate and preempt similar problems with her younger children:

> Art needed help when he was younger with reading. So we really worked with him. Then Tim's teacher sent words home every night. So, when he started reading I just picked up on it from the help I had given Art. Now Jack needs help also, so we've just carried on with him also.

> **Naysmith**
> *Uptown, Maltby*

She does more work with her sons than is specifically called for by the teacher:

> L: I bought those phonics books and reading-writing books, math skills and flash cards, and things like that.
> I: So you've put a lot of time into it. What about the math stuff? Is that the same kind of stuff that the teacher is suggesting that you help with?
> L: No, she hasn't really sent home much for math —more words and reading. I've just followed through with math.

> **Naysmith**
> *Uptown, Maltby*

Helen Moore (Uptown) puts in 10 hours a week doing secretarial work for her school. She is also in the Uptown School's parents' association, contributing considerable time to fund raising and taking students on trips. She and Wayne have three children: Martin, who is 12 and in grade 6, Emily, who is 10 and in grade 4, and Laura, who is 6 and in kindergarten. The older children's homework is routinized, and it is largely self-managed, although their father does give them help with their assignments. The daily routines of the Moore family are busy with a variety of activities:

> Helen: Emily has music lessons on Wednesday and she can't walk. It's out near Ullswater Farms. She takes piano and I have to drive her there. Martin has two paper routes Wednesday and Thursday—just weeklies, but every Wednesday and Thursday. So he gets them together and he goes off on those days. Just until lately, Laura had swimming at 4 o'clock on Monday. So from September to May every Monday night we were at swimming.
>
> I: So you do a lot of running around after school then. So do you eat around six o'clock?
>
> H: We usually eat around 5:30. If I haven't been busy and I'm out with Laura, dinner will be in the oven. If I have been busy, things will be thrown together up here. I find that it is very hectic. Even though I may not have anything at school to do, if it's Christmas or birthdays, even just getting the shopping done there's a lot of running around. Because the kids come home for lunch and they come at 3:30 you have only 2 hours to get things done.

> **Moore**
> *Uptown, Maltby*

Helen views children's television programs as an educational adjunct. Laura watches a children's television program that Helen has the following views on:

> H: [The show is] more than just baby-sitting; it's a good little show with crafts and teaches them how to communicate and how to act. Often times I watch the show. I'm one who always watched TV with my children. I knew exactly what they were watching.
>
> I: Do you still do that?
>
> H: Not as much anymore. With the other children I know what they are watching. I can't sit down and watch everything that they watch but I know what they are watching.

> **Moore**
> *Uptown, Maltby*

Because two of her children are older and are themselves very involved in, and apparently successful in, their work at school, the daily routines that Helen has established do not involve her so directly in educational work. She supervises, and with her husband Wayne, supplies help and advice. The shift into children's self-management of their homework, supported by parental supervision, is a marked feature of this family's school-oriented work day, suggesting a shift in parental role as children grow older from the type of active educational work that we found in Martha Desmond's and Amanda Knight's account to the supervision of children's self-management.

Flexible Routines

Martha Desmond, Amanda Knight and Lisa Naysmith are perhaps the most highly organized of the women who are full-time housewives; Helen Moore is engaged in a pretty intensive regime in which her older children appear to be doing the directly educational work under her and her husband's supervision. By contrast, the mothers we meet in this section adopt more flexible strategies, responding to specific needs, to a child's feelings, or giving her or him time to relax after school. Sally Ames (Uptown), for example, who has five children (all boys, three in elementary school and two under school age) needs greater flexibility:

> They come home about 4:00 and probably the first thing they want to do is they want to have something to eat or drink. And after that with the one boy . . . he was . . . I give him a bit of help with his math when he first comes in. And after that they normally like to watch TV.

Ames
Uptown, Maltby

TV watching is a way of solving some of the problems of managing the activities of children at home. But schoolwork is not neglected. With three boys in school, Sally has to coordinate the different kinds of demands that school imposes. The boys' schoolwork is of different kinds, depending on the child's grade level. All three have work to do at home, particularly reading. Jay's (the oldest, in grade 3) teacher's comments at the last parent-teacher conference indicated that Jay was somewhat below average for his class in mathematics. Sally and her husband Bill decided with the teacher's concurrence to give Jay additional help. Bill is one of the fathers to be described in the following chapter who are directly involved in complementary educational work with their children: Bill undertook working with Jay on his math on Sundays and Sally works with him after school.

Unlike Martha, Amanda, and Lisa, Sally does not initiate educational work that is independent of school demands. She does, however, organize the daily integration of school activities into the school day at home. She watches for the right opportunity to insert a child's schoolwork into the rhythm of his school day: "I find if I catch [Jay] right then before his interest is into anything else then it's easier to get him to sit down and do the work" (Ames, Uptown, Maltby). The required schoolwork has to be built into the home routine. Times of the day are allocated to definite activities. After school, the children may watch TV for a while (with the exception of Jay). After his math is done, however, Jay may watch television with the other children until suppertime. After supper, the children go down into the basement to play or watch television. Sally clears the table and washes the dishes before she reads to them. Television watching is controlled on school days, though less so on weekends. As Sally says, "Saturday is their kind of free day."

Barbara Lindsay has only one son, Chuck, who is 6 and in grade 1 at Downtown School. Though she adjusts the timing to fit Chuck's mood around any work that he brings home from school, she makes sure that it gets done on the day it arrives and is returned when it's due. He brings home three to five sheets of work a day to do.

> I look at it and go over it and if there's a story in it, or something, he's got to read it to me. And tell what he did and go over [inaudible] means he got something wrong and he corrected it. And if it comes back with no stamp then there is something that isn't completed and she [the teacher] writes "homework!" on the top of the page or a note. There's something there that's not right and then I have to change it and he takes it back the next day.
>
> **Lindsay**
> *Downtown School, Maltby*

Chuck's TV watching is controlled. He can watch for an hour while she's making supper, but "He has to do the homework first." There is, however, flexibility in her routine:

> It depends on the day. Everyday is different. Like today he might come home from school and I'll just say to him "Let's see your schoolwork," and I would check it over and he'll read if there is a story involved on the page, he'll read it out to me. Or some of the pages too where they learn their sounds of the letters. So we'll go

over the phonics and how they sound and stuff like that. Sometimes we'll do it when he comes home; it depends on what's going on after school. Like I can tell his mood and he'll sort of say "Mommy, do I have to do it now?" and I'll wait. He will do it after supper. Sometimes we'll wait until my husband comes home and he'll do it with him.

Lindsay
Downtown School, Maltby

Flexibility, however, is within the context of a definite routine:

Barbara: If he has homework he's supposed to do it when he gets home from school.
I: Before he does anything else . . . .
B: His homework is done. Because before he wouldn't do that and then finally, he'd forget about it and the next thing you know you are either doing it right before his bedtime, or leave it, and when he got up in the morning he was doing his homework. I found that was too much of a rush so we just sort of set a rule up that if you have homework you come home and you do it and it's over with and the rest of the evening is yours. Then you don't have to worry about him doing homework.

Lindsay
Downtown School, Maltby

Nancy Gordon (Downtown) experiences a difficulty with supervising and supporting her son Michael's schoolwork. She describes trying to get him to do some homework. Here, the school, or at least the teacher responsible for teaching grade 3, could be seen as working against this parent's efforts. Nancy reports that, according to Michael, the teacher's view is "If you are a good student you don't have to do homework." Nancy, however, doesn't accept this:

Nancy: I guess I feel like I'm overruling the teacher a bit, but I am the parent, and you know at that age the teacher is right and the parents . . . so I try to . . . .
I: [Does] he bring things home from school?
N: Occasionally, occasionally. We are kind of doing it on our own, like he has a chart of how the teacher likes writing. After years, we are not writing correctly, with the way he wants the kids

to learn, so we, you know, take that up, and copy that, and I'll give him times tables to do.
I: So you are doing a lot of this on your own.
N: Yes, yes, just trying to set for the future, when he will do home-work, and time to study for a test and that . . . or Fridays are spelling dictation days—bring your spelling home and we'll go over the words, things like that. Which he does forget sometimes, he forgets a lot.
I: So many things to remember on the way home.
N: Yeah, like the way home.

Gordon
Downtown, Maltby

It is clear that Nancy would like to have schoolwork built into the daily routine, but finds that the ordinary conditions of the day at home don't make it easy.

Michael gets home about 4:10, and there are the other two kids [Vanessa and Joe—respectively 5 and 3] running around. [Vanessa] goes to a playschool twice a week, that's where she is today . . . she is coming probably the same time [as Michael], then too on those two days, so it can be pretty excitable time, but you see he watches a bit of TV first. Then, we do tend to eat din-ner early, then it's clean-up time and we are trying to get a rou-tine where he is doing some schoolwork, whether he is doing some homework, or not, which I find right now, he isn't bring-ing too much home.

Gordon
Downtown, Maltby

It is hard to believe that the lack of support from the teacher does not weaken Nancy and Alec's (her husband's) ability to override Michael's interests in TV, his friends, and other attractions as focuses for his after-school time. She and Alec try to read to the children but do not seem to have succeeded in building reading into the school day as a routine.

Yeah, we try to read stories we get. We think it's good for Michael to practice, reading to the younger kids . . . so he will read to Vanessa. Joe is still squirming. He doesn't want to sit, but we watch. They watch a bit too much TV really. We have—I have—

all kinds of—I should be getting older books now, got all kinds of younger . . . .

Gordon
Downtown, Maltby

Not Strongly School Oriented

The two mothers under this heading are very different from each other, but neither is very strongly oriented towards educational work relevant to school. Patricia Fergus (Uptown) is someone who does not set up clearly defined routines after school for her two daughters: Gloria, in grade 2, and Elizabeth, in kindergarten. She does not take on the kind of managerial role that we have seen described by Martha, Amanda, and Sally. She does not plan: "What I do, it's just natural, it's not planned, I don't say, 'We're going to do this because it's going to teach you.'" In contrast to Martha Desmond who takes up the work that her daughter Carol brings home and contributes her own educational work to the production of Carol's school performance, Patricia Fergus doesn't intervene that way in her daughter Gloria's education. She looks at the work Gloria brings home and praises it, but does not treat it as an occasion for her own educational intervention. Perhaps with her self-consciousness awakened by the interview process, she comments:

> I guess I don't really look as closely as I should be at the papers that Gloria brings home. I don't know . . . I don't know if I'm looking at enough stuff or not.

Fergus
Uptown, Maltby

Elizabeth, the younger child, is at home playing all afternoon. Gloria's after-school routines are self-regulated. She comes home at 3:30 p.m. and goes upstairs and reads, types, and talks to her friends on the phone —Patricia isn't altogether happy about how long she's on the phone. After dinner the chain of events is often similar to the following scenario:

> If it's early, and it will be early enough, they . . . do puzzles, go into the living room sometimes, um, dump out every piece of Lego we own, but they're only allowed in the living room with it so I can sweep it up. So they're there, or they do puzzles on the dining room table, or um, if I've really had enough of them, they

go and get ready for bed early. And then they get their stories and
they each pick out one and Chris [the father] will read to each
one of them or, I like it when he reads 'cause he always puts more
into it, and makes it fun . . . . I just read what it says and that's all,
I don't make it sound like Bert and Ernie or anybody else, so they
have that, and they have time that they can play in their bed, because they have to be in bed by 7:30, and then by 7:45 they are
asleep, so I know that's early but my kids are up early in the
morning too.

Fergus
Uptown, Maltby

Though Patricia is clearly aware of what her daughters are doing after
school, she does not orient her supervision of Gloria's or Liz's after-
school activities with educational objectives in mind. Unusually, however, educationally oriented activities are more actively developed by
Gloria herself, who plays teacher to her younger sister, and by Chris
Fergus, the father, who is the one who looks at Gloria's work after school
and helps her with her assignments, and who reads to the children as
described in the passage above.

Margaret Cartwright is a Downtown School parent, though her husband's professional position (he is a civil engineer) makes their family
household look more like a part of the Uptown School group. Though
she and her husband are both actively involved in their children's development, neither seems to orient to complementary educational work.
Their children are Rebecca, who is 6 and in grade 1, and Philip, who is
only 3. Margaret does not check the work Rebecca brings home from
school everyday; two or three times a week suffices. Rebecca's after-
school routine is relaxed; friends may visit and play two or three times
a week:

Because we are really the first house coming this way, her friends,
when they would come over, usually would stay here. It's easier
for them to stay here than for her to go off to play with somebody
else. So last year it was everyday but now out of realizing I don't
have to do that, either we're busy that night or it is a bit tight or
whatever. I didn't want to get her spoiled into thinking that this
was just an everyday thing. About two or three times a week she

will have a friend over for an hour or so to play with her and Philip is involved too. Otherwise he'll just get so upset. On the other days, she seems to like to get involved, there's always a birthday or something. She likes to make cards. She gets very involved in making cards. She is very good at drawing, and she loves to draw. There are a lot of cousins from my husband's side and she gets into that and if there is no birthday she has those learning books.

Cartwright
Downtown, Maltby

Margaret has observed a tendency in her daughter to become, as she views it, over involved in schoolwork to the point of obsession. It is Rebecca who initiates Margaret's active involvement in complementary educational work and Margaret understands her parental responsibility as training Rebecca to limit her involvement appropriately.

She is so into learning, that like when I remember myself at that age, I was always into dolls . . . . She always takes the books out and she asked me how to do this page. You have to read it. The parent has to be involved in that and I give her a page or two to do because if she does too much she gets so involved that she just doesn't know how to stop. She just has such a curiosity to her. And it seems to be going along with what they are learning at school.

Cartwright
Downtown, Maltby

Margaret does read regularly with Rebecca, but again this does not appear to be school oriented. Rather, she is reading with Rebecca a book, *The Little House on the Prairie*, which she too enjoys. Philip also gets his story, but building blocks with his dad come first. Clearly both Margaret and her husband are doing educational work with their children, but it is not strictly oriented to the school or responsive to the work that Rebecca is sent home with.

Table 4 shows how the various practices of complementary educational work are distributed between the two schools.

Table 4 Patterns of Complementary Educational Work Among Full-Time Housewives: Uptown and Downtown School

Patterns of After-School Educational Work	Uptown School	Downtown School
Educational work as priority	Desmond, Knight,	
Diversified routines	Moore, Naysmith	
Flexible	Ames	Gordon, Lindsay
Not strongly school oriented	Fergus	Cartwright

These groups are ordered with respect to the level of the activity oriented specifically towards school. When educational work is the priority, we find a saturation of the school day with activities oriented towards the development of school-relevant skills. Those characterized as having diversified routines, while clearly actively oriented towards activities complementing the school's educational work, also commit their days to a high level of activity outside school. Those characterized as flexible though active in educational work complementary to the school's are more reactive than proactive and do not show such clearly defined routines as those of the previous two groups. Finally, we have two who differ considerably from each other. Patricia Fergus is not very actively involved with her daughters' schooling. Margaret Cartwright is clearly involved in her children's general educational development but does not appear to be actively oriented to her older daughter's schoolwork. The Fergus household is particularly interesting because, to some extent at least, father Chris and daughter Gloria have taken over some of the educational work that is usually understood as the mother's responsibility.

5

COMPLEMENTARY EDUCATIONAL WORK: EMPLOYED MOTHERS AND FATHERS

In this chapter, we look at the school-oriented work of mothers who are employed, as well as the educational work of fathers. This category includes employed mothers who work full time, as well as those who are employed part time for more than 10 hours per week. Some of those we talked to who work outside the home had variable hours. Paula Jackson (Downtown School), for example, worked as an interviewer in a local mall. When she worked in this capacity, she was on the job full time. But she did not work every day. In addition to the variability of demand for the kinds of surveys she did, her employers adjusted her schedule to her husband's shifts. Carol Irwin's (Downtown School) hours of employment were also vague and variable, largely because she worked in some kind of informal courier service and was on call. In addition to the irregularity of her hours, she also had to be out late into the night. We also have included Susan Heller (Downtown School) in this group. She was not in fact employed, but she was in full-time training as a veterinary assistant and was paying a baby-sitter for her youngest daughter and when her son came home from school. Alice Orton (Uptown School), the only single parent in our group, was employed full time. She paid a neighbor to care for her son when he got home from school and left her younger son with her parents who lived in a nearby city.

For all these mothers, the after-school hours were, in various ways, unavailable or available only intermittently. In what follows, we apply the

EDUCATIONAL WORK AS A PRIORITY

Rather surprisingly, it is Alice Orton (Uptown) who comes closest to the model established for us by Martha Desmond and Amanda Knight. Alice has a professional career and a good job in a large international corporation. Her oldest son Travis, who is 8 years old, attends Uptown School and is in the gifted program. She has been able to pay for and to find exceptionally supportive day care for Travis with a neighbor. Travis walks to his daycare in the morning when Alice leaves for work (taking Simon, her youngest, to her parent's in a nearby city), and goes directly there after school:

> Alice: [The neighbor] is excellent with him. She'll sit down and play checkers with him, or they're into playing Scrabble and Monopoly lately. And they color and draw. She just has one little baby. Her own son, he's 8 months old and she really looks forward to Travis coming home. It's someone to talk to. She's excellent. I've just been so lucky. I feel so fortunate. She really takes a keen interest in him, you know. On his birthday, he walked in and she had balloons and a birthday present, when he went in that morning. So, she is priceless.
> I: Does she talk to him about school?
> A: She does, yes, she sits down and talks about his day and things like that. She's really interested in him so that helps a lot.
> I: And does she tell you about what she's heard from him?
> A: She does, yes. She's excellent about passing on things that she thinks I should know, even if it's just a discipline problem or something of that nature. She's really good. We have a good communication there, so that's good.
>
> **Orton**
> *Uptown, Maltby*

Travis is in the gifted program at Uptown School and is actively interested in his school work, but Alice also does quite a bit of educational work with both Travis and Simon.

> I: What about the kinds of things, about his schoolwork. Does he bring things home?

A: He does, yes.

I: And do you look at it when it comes home?

A: I do yes.

I: What kinds of things do you look for when you look at it?

A: Hmm. Just sort of at the things he's doing. I look to see—he's not a really neat printer: his teacher says he needs a secretary. So I always look for improvements there although I never say anything to him about it too much. I'll just kind of watch to see how he's doing with that. As far as marks go on his tests and things, I don't generally say anything about them. And I think that's probably the last thing that I'd look at. Because, I know he's smart and I know he can do well and I think my main concern is what he's doing.

Orton
Uptown, Maltby

Alice reads to Simon at bedtime and Travis likes to sit beside them:

I try to read them educational books, I don't know why, it's just something within me but, things like teaching them how to count or whatever. And he's [Simon] got one of these tape recorders and I buy him the books and the tape to go along with it. So we'll sit down and put the tape on and we'll go through the book together.

Orton
Uptown, Maltby

"Teaching," she says, "teaching is just part of how I do my mothering."

In various ways, Alice, though a single parent and working full time, is able to contribute considerable educational work to her sons' schooling, in part by hiring others to complement the time she does not have. Moreover Travis at 8, is already beginning to be able to manage his own schooling. Nonetheless, Alice is clearly painstaking and thoughtful in the work she puts into Travis's and Simon's future.

FLEXIBLE ROUTINES

Paula and Gerry Jackson (Downtown) have two children: Merry, who is 7 and in grade 2, and Claudette, who is 3 years old. Paula works outside the home, doing surveys in a nearby mall. Though her work is full time when she is on the job, there are breaks when there is no work to do.

Unfortunately, we didn't get an exact account of how long her breaks were, but her account of her daily routines is in terms of working full time. Her schedule is fitted by her employers both to the school day and to her husband's shifts:

> No, this is the beauty of this job here; they vary my hours. They know that when Gerry is on nights I can work only days, and vice versa. So, say I'm working days down there and Merry comes home at noon, and I'm not here, then—about 11:50—Gerry is, and everything. He usually picks up and might do my dishes or whatever. He's quite a helper. Then he'll get lunch ready for Merry. If I come in, sometimes he'll say to me: "You better go, its 12:00" or whatever. But if I get home around 12:15 and Merry is usually eating her lunch. And I'll just relax and have my coffee and a sandwich or something. And Gerry will say to go up and wash and brush her teeth, which she does. She brushes her hair and she is off.

> **Jackson**
> *Downtown, Maltby*

Despite the flexibility of Paula's hours, one way or another, she's absent during part of the after-school time that nonemployed mothers are able to dedicate to educational routines, should they choose to do so. She is at work in the afternoon or in the evening. In any case, educational work is not a marked priority for Merry's after-school routine:

> Well if it's a nice day, she'll come in hungry of course, and get a snack. She likes to watch her Thunder Cats . . . . It's a cartoon from 4:00 to 4:30. Sometimes she'll watch it. Other times if it's nice out she comes in and grabs her skipping rope. There are kids out there and they play. You have to call her in at 5:30 or 5:45 for supper. It depends on what kind of a day it is.
> I: So after dinner, what kinds of things happen?
> Paula: Well if she needs to have a bath, sometimes she'll go up and run one. Sometimes you'll have to tell her to. I'm still washing her hair [inaudible] after supper and if it's nice out she'll go outside. Once in a while we'll play a game together. We do things like go for walks and stuff if it's nice out.

> **Jackson**
> *Downtown, Maltby*

Paula contrasts the present with the period she spent as a full-time housewife when she was able to spend time with Merry doing the same kind of educational work that has been described above by Martha Desmond and Amanda Knight:

> I enjoyed when Merry was little [before Paula started her interviewing job], teaching her like preschool, the alphabet and all that. She does have a good start in school. The teacher said so. And I'd like to have that time with Claudette too. Maybe if I hadn't had it with Merry, but I did . . . . I taught her the alphabet by making up these little cards with the a's and b's and c's and stuff —and then eventually getting her to write them. First of all teaching her that song, a, b, c, d, e, f, g . . . I started out with that, then making up the little cards and then making little pictures like of an apple and showing her the "a." I made up a lot of those cards, thousands of them. And then . . . it's hard to remember back that far. Claudette isn't as enthused as Merry was, reading books, showing her pictures, all kinds of stuff.

Jackson
Downtown, Maltby

Fran Ecker's daughter Ellen is 7 and in grade 2 at Downtown School. There are two younger children: Ben, who is 4 and in preschool, and Miranda, who is 2. Fran has a full-time secretarial job. The two younger children are in childcare with a friend of Fran's who lives just across the street. Ellen goes to the same childcare when she comes home from school unless her father, Bob, who is on shift work at Big Plant (a major manufacturing enterprise in the area), is at home during the day—in which case she comes straight home:

> I: Do they do any schoolwork before dinner?
> Fran: Sometimes, not usually.
> I: So who would oversee this, Bob?
> F: Yes, or Ellen would do it and show it to me. They don't really have any homework.
> I: Does she do any extra work around school? Little extra things that are connected somehow to school, or does she just do homework if it comes home and school work at school?
> F: Oh no, she does things here. She's always trying to write things out and stuff. She really likes school.

I: Does she.
F: So far.

Ecker
Downtown, Maltby

Much of Fran's educational concerns and efforts go into her son Ben who has a speech problem. Fran feels that it's important that he improve considerably before going into kindergarten, but she still finds it difficult to keep up with the regular 15 minute per day exercise recommended by the professional they consulted. "Sometimes [it gets done], sometimes not. It just depends what's going on here and if he's tired." Fran is, of course, not available in the immediate after-school hours and Ellen seems to be pretty much on her own when it comes to school work.

NOT STRONGLY SCHOOL ORIENTED

Though Susan Heller (Downtown) is not, strictly speaking, in full-time employment, she is currently full time in a training program for animal care. She has two children: Peter, who is age 7 in grade 1, and Stephanie, who is 3. Peter and Stephanie are cared for by a baby-sitter who comes to their home. Peter, however, is rather left to his own devices in the after-school hours and spends the time playing with friends. Susan does not seem to be very active in relation to his schooling:

> He doesn't talk much about his school; he comes home, shows me his work, and if he's got something wrong I'll say, "How come you didn't get this one right?" And he'll say, "I don't know." . . . When Cindy was baby-sitting I never saw any of his work . . . because he'd bring it home and they'd shove it into the drawer and then I'd never, they wouldn't tell me about it. But Norm (the current baby-sitter), he sets it up on top of the fridge and when he's leaving he'll say, "Peter's work on top of the fridge, eh." He brings home a list of words he's got to learn and you've got to sign them, or he'll bring something home he has to read to you, you sign it and he takes it back.
> I: You do sign it though. So that they know that the parent . . .
> Susan: That he's read it to you and that he's read it correctly, like I make him read it until he's got it all right. Then he brings home a list of words and they get a star or so many points, and they take that back to school and they say all the words out loud. He brings

that home about once a week. The last one he brought home he spilt milk all over it.

Heller
Downtown, Maltby

Susan does not read to Peter. Although he picked up reading early and apparently reads well for his own pleasure, she does not believe in reading to the children.

> I: Do you read to him?
> S: No he reads his own books. I've never read to them, I figure when they learn how to read, then they're not going to learn to read by me reading to them, so they've got to learn to read on their own. Like I know a lot parents will say well you should read to your kids a story at night. Why, you really can't. To me, if you read them a bedtime story before they go to bed, they dream about that story, you know, and say you're reading something like Goldilocks and the Three Bears, or something, you know, they're going to dream about three bears coming after them.
> I: Well a lot of those stories have some violence in them, so I can see that.
> S: Well I figure if they want to read, let them learn to read and let them alone. Now if he wants something read to him, fine, I'll read it to him, or if he gets stuck on a word he'll ask me what it is, but I've never read to them.

Heller
Downtown, Maltby

And, in fact, this seems to have been how Peter learned to read:

> S: The teacher was surprised he picked [reading] up so quickly. Like he reads, and he can write sentences. And the teacher said to me, when we went for the interview there, before he got his report card, and she asked me. And I said he picked it up just like that, reading eh? And I said: "Well he watched—he was in [nursery] school . . . for 2 and 3 and junior kindergarten when he was 4 and kindergarten when he was 5.

Heller
Downtown, Maltby

Far from contributing educational work to her son's schooling, if anything, her relation to her son's school work is a negative one. When they moved to Maltby, Peter had already spent several months in kindergarten and in his new school, the teacher wanted to move him directly into grade 1. Susan, however, said "No!" Her sister had found first grade difficult when she was advanced early into it, and so Peter has done kindergarten twice and is only now in first grade.

Carol Irwin (Downtown) is another who is not very actively involved in the educational work that contributes to her child's schooling. She has one child, Jasmine, who is 7 and in grade 2. She does not have a regular job but is earning income by taking on various odd jobs with varying hours, sometimes working in the evening and running late into the night.

> I: Does she bring homework home?
> Carol: Oh, yes. She finished and I'll hear her say "I've got to take it back." Because Jasmine didn't bring home all her papers from school. She left them everything in her desk and she had to [garbled] her desk. [Garbled] a lot of papers like that. And I wondered where all her homework was.
> I: You mean she hadn't been bringing it home.
> C: Well sometimes they do folders, you know, and they don't bring it home for quite a long time so I didn't question it . . . they do like a book . . . . It could be a spring thing coming up and they do this book, right? And they put all their work into it . . . . Nothing comes home. Except for the odd sheet, right? . . . . And this was what happening so I never questioned it. Well she brought home these papers that were all loose. And I, my husband and I, sat there and looked through them all, just to check the work because of this new teacher. And . . . here was all these sheets [inaudible] work, empty!

> **Irwin**
> *Downtown, Maltby*

Carol is not always able to be at home before Jasmine gets home from school, and when she is, school matters do not get automatic priority:

> I: So when she comes home . . . when you come home, do you just talk about school, or—or you know, look at her work at that time?
> C: Yes . . . . If I haven't got company or I'm not busy at that moment, when she comes in the door, I usually say to her . . . . "How

come you are so late coming in?" or something, you know. And then I will say to her "How did school go?," "How did your day go?," you know. If she has been in school all day and hasn't come home for lunch, I say to her "How did your day go in school?," "Did you do okay?," or . . . . "Have a hard time?" or . . . some days she used to come in the door, she used to come in mad, "Did you have a bad day?." . . .. And the conversation is just brief and then she will give me her school work. And she may have a note or something and she will say "Sign it right now" or "I need the money for tomorrow" or . . . . And I will say "Do you have any homework?" usually later on after I think about it. She's gone up-stairs . . . . I'll send her up to her room . . . and then her home-work and she sits right over there where you are because the TV is here and her dad's usually watching TV. And this is like this and she's not paying any attention. So I have to put her over there, so . . . she has a desk in her room . . . .

Irwin
Downtown, Maltby

Though Carol is attentive to Jasmine, she does not contribute educational time. She "lets" Jasmine read, but does not read to her.

SUMMARY

The following table (Table 5) shows us the variety of educational routines by mothers who are employed full-time.

With the exception of Alice Orton, the mothers we talked to who were putting substantial time into their employment (or training) were, on the whole, much less able to contribute time and thought to their children's schooling. The empty category—diversified routines—is striking. Under the heading "Full-Time Housewives" (chapter 4), we described two families that combined strong supports of their children's education with a commitment to a variety of other activities such as sports, swimming, and piano lessons that took up family time in the evenings. Examination of the mothering stories of employed women suggests that women who are employed outside the home are less able to make the kind of contributions of educational work time that we saw described by those who were full-time housewives. Nor are they able to make an on-going commitment to activities that are not either school- or home-oriented. Alice Orton is an exception, but Alice earns a professional salary and has also been lucky enough to find—and pay for—childcare

Table 5 Patterns of Complementary Educational Work Among Employed Mothers: Uptown and Downtown School

Patterns of after-school educational work	Uptown School	Downtown School
Educational work as priority	Orton	
Diversified routines		
Flexible routines		Ecker, Jackson
Not strongly school oriented		Heller, Irwin

for Travis that provides him with educational supports that supplement the time she manages, somehow, to put in with her strenuous schedule.

Though time is not the only factor at work here, as can be seen in the accounts that Susan Heller and Carol Irwin provided, its significance is emphasized by Paula's story of the kind of educational work she put in with her eldest daughter before she went back to full-time employment. If we had interviewed her during that period of her life, the educational work she was doing with her daughter would have looked very much like that of Martha Desmond and Amanda Knight.

FATHERS' INVOLVEMENT IN COMPLEMENTARY EDUCATIONAL WORK

We argued in chapter 1 that the traditional organization of the middle-class family creates the conditions under which women's work is made available to support their children's schooling and their children's schools. The mothering discourse certainly assigns to women the major role in the work of sustaining their children in school, at least at the elementary level. In both Downtown and Uptown Schools, we found that the husbands of the women we talked to, with one exception, played a marginal role in the complementary educational work of the family. Most fathers, in both groups, are described as being involved and interested, but not as directly participating in complementary educational work. Helen Moore's account is typical:

I: Does your husband help with, is he involved in the children's schoolwork at all?
Helen: Well at this stage [Emily] is in grade 1. [Wayne] always checks all her work too. Last week he had a busy week. I had my swimming so I had to go out and on Wednesday he has his class and then Thursday he had a meeting. And I thought I didn't really

want the papers hanging around the table, which I normally keep them on the table until he comes home so he sees them and then he puts them in the basket. So I assumed that he didn't see them but he had gone up into the basket to look at the work. So he is interested. He always checks it.

Moore
Uptown School

Wayne does, however, help his older children with their assignments:

H: He's involved. In fact, he's the one when they have an assignment, especially our eldest does not like you to lean over his shoulder and help him. We can get into great rows when I try to assist. Alan can work with him better than I can. Martin and I are very much alike as far as emotions are concerned and we take everything very personally. This is right . . . what do you mean it isn't right? Wayne works better with him and when it comes to a project, an essay or a speech, he oftentimes is the one who will take him under tow. He enjoys it more; he can collect his thoughts better than I can. He can articulate and help the kids but he will not do it for them.

Moore
Uptown, Maltby

Helen Moore, however, does adopt a kind of supervisory role:

Oftentimes it's very distressing. They'll do it and he'll say that's not good enough and they'll have to start all over again. That's very frustrating. I'll whisper to him that it's their project—do you think you could let them do it? It's not that he does it but he'll watch and if this isn't straight and something's not right he forgets.

Moore
Uptown, Maltby

It may well be that fathers are more likely to be involved in complementary educational work as their children get older. However, fathers' involvement in both Downtown and Uptown Schools was, as we would expect, sharply limited by their jobs and was generally minimal compared with that of mothers. The women we talked to also clearly viewed themselves as central to the educational project. They described their husbands as "helping" or as backup when they were overloaded. Few fathers in either group had much time available to be active otherwise.

Of the seven families we visited in the Downtown School area, five of the fathers worked at Big Plant. They worked shifts. The one Uptown School father who worked shifts found that his work interfered with his ability to contribute to his child's education. By contrast with the Uptown School fathers whose hours were regularly extended into the early evening by lengthy travel time, Downtown School fathers were, at least intermittently (depending on their shifts) at home and awake when the child or children came home from school, and they participated, in some form or other, in complementary educational work: "when my husband is on days it's usually my husband who'll read [Tony] a story . . . [Larry] usually gets two weeks that he's on days and he'll go up and maybe read him something . . . " (Lindsay, Downtown School).

Nancy Gordon described her husband, Alec, as providing pretty much the same kinds of education support to their son Michael as she does. His shift work means that he's not always able to be involved, but when he is involved with Michael in "reading and the times tables," Barbara Lindsay deploys her husband's contributions as back up to her flexible strategies of managing their son's schoolwork.

> Everyday day is different. Like today [Tony] might come home from school and I'll just say to him "Let's see your schoolwork," and I would check it over and he'll read—if there is a story involved on the page, he'll read it out to me. So we'll go over the phonics and how they sound and stuff like that. Sometimes we'll do it when he comes home, it depends on what's going on after school. Like I can tell his mood and he'll sort of say "Mommy, do I have to do it now" and I'll wait. He will do it after supper. Sometimes we'll wait until my husband comes home and he'll do it with him.
>
> **Lindsay**
> *Downtown School*

Uptown School fathers are, for the most part, simply not present and available to do the after-school work that appears to be central to the complementary educational work of mothers with children in both Downtown and Uptown Schools. Margaret Cartwright, whose husband, Ellis, is the only one in the Downtown School group who is a professional (a civil engineer), describes the change introduced into their family routines when Ellis took a job in nearby Major City:

Margaret: At first the children didn't understand why but then I explained to them that because daddy is going to Major City and coming back later, we're eating later so if you can have your pajamas on and that. Well sometimes we're eating and it's quarter to 7:00, and there's not that much time after, and he wanted to spend a bit of time. I know some moms talk about getting their kids to bed at 7:00, but we can't seem to get around to that because first of all Philip is waiting all day to build a house with Ellis so he has to build a house and Ellis get right involved in that and then they both want their stories . . .
I: Does Rebecca tell Ellis about her school day?
M: Yes, he asks her how things have gone. He's very interested in what's going on in her day. I think he feels the difference too from last year being there and seeing everything. So he really wants to know. He hasn't seen them from the day before so it's from mealtime to mealtime. He's really good. He's great with the kids and I don't have to get him involved, he just does it.

Cartwright
Downtown School

Only two of the Uptown School fathers were described as being regularly and directly involved in educational work. Bill Ames works with his son, Jay, on weekends:

I: Is your husband involved in the children's school work at all?
Sally: He has helped the one boy an awful lot with his reading and also with his math too because, whereas I'm probably more by the book, and I want it done a certain way, my husband can kind of make more of a game of it, and usually my husband has a different way of showing it to them too, but he is pretty good that way.
I: So when does he help? On the weekends or does he help at night or?
S: Normally, I would have to say it would have to be on a Sunday. 'Cause he doesn't get home until 6:00 or 6:30 at night [so] he doesn't have that much time at night.

Ames
Uptown School

Chris Fergus, who is a general contractor and apparently has a more flexible schedule than some of the other Uptown School fathers, spends time with his daughter Gloria, both going over her schoolwork and helping her with assignments.

A number of the fathers are described as being involved in reading to their children. Unlike the complementary educational work that picks up directly on a child's schoolwork and which appears mostly to be done during the afternoon or early evening of the school day, bedtime reading doesn't appear to be so clearly seen as the mother's responsibility. Uptown School fathers are more likely to be reported as involved in evening reading to their children than Downtown School fathers.[1] Martha Desmond, whose daughter Carol attends Uptown School, describes evening reading as shared by herself and her husband, Ray.

> Martha: We have a bedtime story every night.
> I: And how do you go about it?
> M: One for each of them or maybe three books together. It just depends on . . . if Ray is home he reads to Billy and I'll read to Carol or we'll switch. I'll take Billy and he'll take Carol. We read a story every night.
>
> **Desmond**
> *Uptown School*

Even including bedtime reading, Uptown School fathers are not, in general, reported as being actively involved in educational work that can be viewed as directly complementary to their children's schooling. As noted above, Bill Ames (Uptown) is the only father reported to be regularly involved in educational work with his child. However, a number of the mothers we talked to described the fathers' involvement with children as contributing important, but not strictly educational, values to their children. Amanda Knight expresses her sense of the value of a division of educational work in which she does more of the teaching, while Joseph contributes in the following ways:

> [Joseph] teaches them the fun things in life. I guess maybe fathers often do that. He'll play basketball with them. He'll play football. Or he does the gardening in the garden and they go out and they'll plant seeds and things. And he'll often take them to the park and things like that or up to the cottage by themselves.
>
> **Knight**
> *Uptown School*

Similarly, Fran Ecker reports that her husband Bob takes the children fishing and Ellis, Margaret Cartwright's husband, builds houses with his son Philip when he comes home in the evening (see above quote).

In terms of educational work that is complementary to the school's work, we graded the fathers in terms of the level of involvement that their wives reported. If they were described as reading to the child or helping in some way with the child's schoolwork, they are assigned to the *active* category in the table below; if they were reported only as looking at the work a child brought home from school or being interested in what she or he has been doing at school, they are described as *interested, but not active*. It must be remembered that the categories created here are based on incidental reporting, as this was not a central topic at the time of research; it is perfectly possible that the information is simply missing because the topic was not pursued very actively in the interviews.

Though the fathers in both Downtown and Uptown Schools are represented as being interested and involved in their children's education, their contribution, with some exceptions,[2] is significantly limited by lack of coordination of their work schedules with the school day. Those activities in which they are involved with their children are less directly complementary to the children's work at school: reading, sports, gardening, fishing, playing checkers, and building houses with blocks, for example, are all ways in which fathers are involved with their children and can be fitted into fathers' paid work schedules. In some respects, though intermittently, we have seen that Downtown School fathers are more available to contribute educational work directly complementing the daily school routine than Uptown School professional fathers.

In general, despite these variations, fathers on the whole contribute little to the overall educational work done at home that directly complements the work of the school. The major responsibility belongs to the mothers.

Table 6 Fathers' Involvement in Complementary Educational Work: Uptown and Downtown Schools

Level of Involvement	Uptown School	Downtown School
Active	Ames, Desmond, Fergus, Gordon, Jackson, Lindsay Moore, Naysmith	
Interested but not active	Knight	Cartwright, Ecker, Heller, Irwin

CONCLUSION

In the previous chapter, we looked at different patterns of complementary educational work among women who were full-time housewives. In this chapter, we have addressed the variations in the educational work of employed mothers and fathers that are directly complementary to the work of teachers in their children's schools. As we've emphasized, we're not concerned with families' contributions to the achievement of individual children, but with the kind of contribution made, through the child, to the school's educational work. Of course, these two contributions aren't wholly separable. A child's achievement is within a given educational context. Nonetheless, our aim is to look at the relationship between a family's economic situation, particularly the claims on the mother's time, and the kinds of contributions mothers and fathers make to educational work at home that complements the work of the school. We can first look at the contributions made by mothers, whether full-time housewives or employed, in terms of the different patterns of complementary educational work they contribute to each school. Table 7 combines the families from both schools in terms of the different patterns of educational work we identified among them. When we do so, striking differences between the two schools become visible as are illustrated in the following table:

Table 7 Patterns of Complementary Educational Work Among Employed Mothers and Fathers: Uptown and Downtown School

Patterns of After-School Educational Work	Uptown School	Downtown School
Educational work as priority	Desmond, Knight (Orton)[3]	
Diversified routines	Moore, Naysmith	
Flexible	Ames	Gordon, Lindsay, Ecker, Jackson
Not strongly school oriented	Fergus	Cartwright, Heller, Irwin

As can be seen, all those who either give priority to educational work in the home in the organization of the family's daily routine or whose routines are similar except that more time is given (for example, to sports) have children in Uptown School. By contrast all those who do not or are not able to make the same kind of commitment of time have children in Downtown School. Only one of the mothers of the children at Uptown School is working full time whereas, of the Downtown school mothers, four of the seven are employed outside the home. Striking too, is that three of the four women who appear not to be very active in their child or children's schooling, three are Downtown School parents.

Of course, nothing decisive can be read from this table alone. The numbers are much too small. But the stories themselves do exhibit how the conditions under which full-time housewives do educational work differ from those under which women who are employed outside the home work. For the latter group, the times of day when full-time housewife mothers are heavily involved in educational work are those that are unavailable for most of those mothers working outside the home. Alice Orton is the exception here, but she is able to pay to supplement her own input of educational time. We can see very clearly in all these accounts just what is involved in *work* that is done in the home for the daily care and education of children. A work life outside the home takes energy and thought; so does the kind of educational work that women like Martha Desmond and Amanda Knight contribute, let alone other aspects of household work and childcare. Helen Moore and Lisa Naysmith described for us families focused rather differently than the first two, but no less highly organized or tense, as in Helen's case. Just as vividly, we can see in Paula Jackson's and Fran Ecker's accounts the ways in which a flexible management of the educational work of the school day responds to the realities of outside work schedules as well as the division of energies and thought between home and paid work. Such differences are, we argue, consequential for the schools that the children from these different family situations attend.

The information we gathered about fathers was not categorizable in the same way. All except the absent Mr. Orton were employed full-time. So we compared fathers only in terms of whether they had been described as active in the complementary educational work or just interested in their children's schooling. The differences between Uptown and Downtown Schools are enhanced by considering those fathers who could be described as being actively involved. Our data suggests that Uptown School benefits more than does Downtown School from family time dedicated to complementary educational work: In the Desmond, Moore, and Naysmith families—all with children at Uptown School—both mother and father are making significant contributions of time to educational work; and while Gordan, Lindsay, and Ecker (fathers with children in Downtown School) are active, the overall pattern of family routines as described by their wives does not give educational work a priority.

We cannot, of course, reason from this very small group to the larger population of the communities served by the two schools, but we can find the everyday life correlates of what we will hear described in the following chapter from the point of view of teachers and administrators.

6

UPTOWN AND DOWNTOWN IN MALTBY: SCHOOL AND BOARD PERSPECTIVES

In the previous chapters, we have retold mothers' stories about the different kinds of work that they do for their children's schooling. Mothers' educational and managerial work—their discursive understandings of mothering, their coordination of uncoordinated family schedules, and their household pedagogy—mediates their children's participation in the everyday lives of schools. Embedded in their stories are descriptions of the schools in Turner's Crossing and Maltby. They present educators and their schools as relating differently to parents in middle-class and working-class areas. In Maltby, we were able to interview the school administrators, both principals and vice principals, and the superintendent and assistant superintendents at the level of the board. Their practices and policies recognize and build on the different kinds of contributions that parents, principally mothers, make to the operation of the schools in different situations of middle- and working-class communities. Parents' contributions to the work of schooling provide the conditions under which educational policies are put into practice in the actualities of particular school districts.

Our interviews with mothers were oriented to the daily features of their work for schooling—beginning in women's experience in order to explore the social relations of educational inequality. Our interviews with teachers and administrators were structured differently. We were interested in their experiences of working with parents and with the administrative implications of different kinds, or levels, of parental involvement in schooling. Our interview questions stayed close to their everyday work in education, but they were generated from our interviews with mothers.

Neighborhoods, or school catchments, tend to be home to particular categories of families—*single parent families, poor families, good families, middle-class families,* and so on. Family homes reflect the economic resources that are available to them. The characterizations of families by educators are built on those typified economic resources, *as well as on the family work that is available to the school.* Educators' descriptions of families and communities support the different reputations of schools, the various work processes of teachers and administrators in different schools, and they rationalize the different student outcomes that are a feature of schooling.

From the perspective of the school, the individual work of mothers is viewed as parental concern, support, and involvement, and these descriptions are generalized to neighborhoods and communities. There is a narrow band of acceptable parental activities that are visible to teachers. According to research conducted in Louisiana, in both white and black neighborhoods, teachers defined parental involvement in terms of classroom and school needs. Parental involvement that did not fit within those boundaries was invisible to teachers and administrators (St. John, Griffith, & Allen-Haynes, 1997; see also Lareau & Horvat, 1999 for a description of similar processes in Pennsylvania). Restricted conceptions of parents and their involvement in schools appear also in the interviews with both mothers and educators in this study. As we will show, these conceptions are not simply patterns of beliefs held by educators, but rather, they are actual activities that coordinate institutional action between the school and the families in the surrounding neighborhood. This institutional coordination reproduces the social inequalities fundamental to schooling.

In this chapter, we explore the ways in which teachers, schools, and school board administrators coordinate their work with the work of parents. Manicom's studies (1988, 1995) examine the concordance of parental and teacherly work in the kinds of classroom-relevant competencies that children have, or have not, acquired in the home. Our course of inquiry took a different direction. We were concerned to learn from educators about the ways in which they connected with parents. So too, we wanted to find out how they appraised the implications of various familial backgrounds for the educational objectives of the school. Teachers and administrators, in response to our questions, told us about their experience of working with parents and of the implications of different kinds or levels of parental work for schooling.

Interviews with teachers and administrators followed somewhat different paths and produced rather different kinds of stories. Teachers talked about how they connected with parents, the pressures parents did or did not put on teachers, the kinds of guidance they sought to give, and how they went about dealing with problems that arose. Teachers and administrators, when talking to us about their classrooms and how parents contributed to their work in that setting, also reflected on the characteristics of the neighborhoods from which the children were drawn. This topic was even more central to administrators both at the level of the school and of the board. There were stereotypes, for example, of single parent families (illustrated by terms such as *broken homes*) and middle-class families, but clearly such stereotypes, accurate or not, reflected the working realities within which their work as administrators was done. Educators' descriptions of families and communities support the different reputations of schools, the various work processes of teachers and administrators in different schools, and the family work that is available to the school.

TEACHERS

Teachers depend on parents' work for the smooth running of their classroom. They depend particularly on a parent's readiness to give time when their child's work at school begins to fall behind the teacher's expectations for the class, or when there are problems in her or his classroom behavior. We asked teachers what kind of difference it would make to their teaching if they had classes half the size of their present class (those we spoke to had classes of 23 or 24; one of the Downtown School classes was larger). All the teachers responded that smaller class sizes would enable them to give more individualized attention to children. Falling back on parents for additional supplementary teaching is a way of handling developmental differences in individual children. For example, the Uptown grade 1 teacher talked to us about how she sees, in her class at the beginning of the year, developmental differences between those born early and later in the school year.

Teachers in both Uptown and Downtown Schools describe working with parents in similar ways. They meet with parents both at the beginning of the year and again when report cards are due; they send home material that children have produced in class for parents to check; they ask for parental help and support when there are problems, whether academically or behaviorally. However, there are differences as well between the practices of the two schools. What Uptown School teachers send home with the children tends to call for parental involvement in a task, whereas Downtown teachers seem not to take for granted the active involvement of parents. Downtown's grade 2–3 teacher merely packages up the children's work with his comments and sends it home with the child every Monday. The grade 1 teacher is more interactive; she finds parents helpful and supportive and sends things home with children for parents to read with them (she also sends out her own classroom newsletter once a month). Downtown's kindergarten teacher seems to involve parents when there are problems with a child's work: If she feels a child is having difficulty, she writes a note to or phones the parents to "ask if they could give them a little help." She gives the following example:

> The child yesterday did a paper with numbers on it and was having a great deal of difficulty recognizing from eleven to twenty. So I said that they were doing fine up to ten, could they get a little extra help at home from eleven to twenty. The paper is pinned on the child and goes home with the child.
>
> **Kindergarten Teacher**
> *Downtown*

She does not, however, work interactively with the parent as was reported by some of the Uptown School teachers. When she meets with parents around the report cards, she tries to encourage parents to be involved:

> I may show them some little games or activities that they could do at home to help the child. I find, for example, learning the abc's, they [the children] can sing me the song, but if I point to individual letters all mixed up, they don't know them. So I'll give the parents some ideas of games and little things they can do to help their child learn the abc's.
>
> **Kindergarten Teacher**
> *Downtown*

The kindergarten teacher gives suggestions, but again, there is no expectation that the parent will in some way provide the teacher with evidence of how she or he is taking up the suggestions.

Uptown School teachers appear to be more demanding, and expect parents to respond in some way when material is sent home. The

Uptown grade 1 teacher we talked to describes sending home "things for them to read" but has adopted a procedure that checks as much on the mother as on the child:

> I ask them every once in a while, maybe once a week, I send home something that the child is to read to the mother and she is to sign it and return it. And I have a good response . . . . And [I send a] word list and so on that she can practice with them and then they return it. And if I find that they've done something and have a lot of errors, I'll say "he needs help in this area." They'll usually send it back.
>
> **Grade 1 Teacher**
> *Uptown*

Uptown's grade 2 teacher will check for reasons if a child doesn't bring back the booklet she took home duly signed by the parent:

> I have one little girl—I feel very sorry for her—that should be taking [the booklet] home every night and getting it signed. A lot of the kids, they've had about 2–3 weeks of this already and a lot of them have a full page of stickers. After the first couple of days . . . Alice hadn't brought the booklet back and I asked her about it. She said: "My mom says we really don't have time to do this." That's being very honest and things are maybe not as smooth or maybe they're going through a [period of adjustment] . . . And I'm wondering if mom's working full time, which I am too. I'm a working mom.
>
> **Grade 2 Teacher**
> *Uptown*

Uptown's kindergarten teacher not only sends home a variety of children's classroom products, but also often incorporates tasks for the children to do with their parents. She prepares materials that the child can take home and read to a parent or parents:

> Some of the things they take home, they read to their moms and dads. We do a lot of booklets. An apple is green. A grasshopper is green, and they have spelled *green* in the booklet themselves and I've printed the rest so they read it to their mom and dad . . . that's something they memorize . . . . They take it home and they

read it to their mom. So all year I do a lot of that with them. And so it satisfied the parents; [they] realize that they [the children] are doing a lot of reading things.

Kindergarten Teacher
Uptown

Uptown's grade 3 teacher described the material she sends home for parents to work on with their children. She consciously designs it both to coordinate with current classroom focus but also so that it fits into the parents' busy schedules:

Most of the time it's reading or rereading the stories I have for comprehension—small stories on cards with questions on them and the mothers sit with the child; the child reads it and the mother asks the questions. I try to keep it as simple as possible because a lot of parents have a very full day too, and with this age group anything that goes over fifteen minutes is very unfair.

Kindergarten Teacher
Uptown

Sometimes parents jump the gun, according to Uptown's grade 2 teacher:

And the kid's come back and said to me "My mom's making me do math every night because I had four wrong on that last sheet" and really they don't need to do math at all.
I: How do you handle something like that?
T: Well, with the little girl that it happened to, I explained to her that she was getting more mistakes now that her mom was help-ing her and she really didn't need the help, and if, you know, she wanted to do extra work, I could give her a book. Her mom was making up the questions for her and I could give her a book and her mom would like that, you, the questions wouldn't be as dif-ficult as mom was making. So she went home and told her mom (laughter) and told her that I said she didn't need the math help, and she, the mom, sort of stopped and didn't ask for a book.

Grade 2 Teacher
Uptown

This teacher doesn't have to invite parents to do their supplemental work; parents are already at work behind the scenes, as we have seen, picking up on what they see as problems with their children's work and doing their best to remedy it.

Both Downtown and Uptown teachers give special help when a child is having problems. The Downtown grade 2–3 teacher describes how he's working with the mom in relation to one boy that's getting nowhere in his reading: "So then I call mom, and she came in and she's concerned, so I give her an extra copy of all the lessons, and he re-does them at home." The Uptown grade 3 teacher works closely with parents around children who are dropping behind the class in a particular area. Her approach, however, is characteristically more interactive:

> I gave one of the parents a phonics work book and acetate sheets and a washable marker. I asked her to start at a certain page in the book and I checked off the pages that I wanted her to work on and I asked for her to bring them [the acetate sheets] back and then we wash them off at school, then send them home again. And I would check more pages and send them home. With another fellow, I sent home some readers from a [no name] series, with some open-ended questions for her to do some reading with him.
>
> **Grade 3 Teacher**
> *Uptown*

She also described, with approval, a mom who was extremely concerned about her child who was having problems. According to the grade 3 teacher, the mother did an excellent job working with him, clearly in consultation with his classroom teacher.

If the mothers of children in Uptown School appear to be more actively engaged than those of Downtown School children, they also appear to take more initiative and to exert more pressure on teachers. Parents are active not only in the kind of supplementary educational work described in chapter 4, they are also, according to Uptown School teachers, directly active in attempting to influence or control their child's school experience. In this way, they are like middle-class parents described in other settings who put pressure on the school to educate their children in ways that are congruent with the family's educational goals (Griffith, 1984; Lareau, 1987). Uptown School teachers feel that they are under scrutiny from parents. Parents, in various ways, may attempt to exert control over what is happening to their children in the school.

There's an essential contradiction between the particularistic relationship a parent has to her or his child and the institutional forms of appraisal of that child in the context of a group of children whose work and development is being appraised by a teacher. Uptown's grade 3 teacher expressed this issue from an educator's viewpoint:

> I know that every child is important to that parent, but you, as a teacher, sometimes have to give a child more attention than others, and it may not be their child. I think that's a very difficult area. I also think that sometimes people find it hard to accept their child for what their child might be academically or socially or otherwise, and I think those people sometimes make it difficult. They feel that you have something against the child personally when you say that there is a problem.
>
> **Grade 2 Teacher**
> *Uptown*

The exercise of initiative by parents appears to be much more a feature of the Uptown School teachers' experiences than it is of teachers at Downtown School. One Uptown School teacher, who has developed elaborate booklets that both represents children's work to parents and encourages children to practice their skills with parents, goes so far as to say that "Half the time the game you're playing when you're teaching is keep the parents off your back, and then you can get on with educating the kid . . . . If parents could only wait for it to happen," she adds, after giving an account of her method of teaching, reading, and writing, which presumably does not conform to the expectations of the parents. Her comments, and those from other Uptown teachers, suggest that, in general, they work with parents who are actively involved in and concerned about how the school is educating their children. For example, an Uptown grade 1 teacher we talked to described the pressure she experiences from parents whose child came into the Reading Readiness program of the first grade: "You really have to have a good rapport with his or her parents, because they are on your doorstep quite a lot," and she adds as a general characterization that "parents are so protective."

Downtown School teachers do not seem to experience much, if any, academic pressure from parents. A second- and third-grade teacher describes his experience discussing academic or behavioral problems with parents:

They sort of want us to tell them what we're going to do. Okay? Whether they understand it or not, they sort of trust that we're going to do it . . . so long as I let them know that I know "here's what we're going to do about it," they seem to be happy.

Grade 2–3 Teacher
Downtown

He also describes working selectively with a child who is having difficulties, depending on whether the parents are willing to give their support to his efforts.

These differences in the teacher-parent or teacher-mother relationship seem more than differences between the individual parents that the school is working with. We have already noticed (in chapter 4) Nancy Gordon's concerns that her grade 3 son does not bring work home regularly, and her and her husband's attempts to work with him on their own. We may also note that she does not apparently feel that it's appropriate for her to contact the teacher or the principal to raise this issue. Everything we learned from the classroom teachers we spoke to at Uptown School showed us that teachers' practices are aimed at, and avoid precisely, such challenges to their teaching practices, and that Uptown parents who had concerns such as Nancy's would not hesitate to take them up with the school.

The differences between the schools are striking. They can be summarized in terms of the different ways in which teachers and parents interact around the schooling process. Uptown teachers are actively engaged with parents, particularly when there are problems. Downtown teachers, while informing parents, making the children's work available for parents to scrutinize, and providing parents with materials to work with when their children are having problems, do not describe interacting with parents around children's academic problems (such as preparing materials specifically for parent-child educational work) taking for granted that parents will be active educationally, and so on. Downtown School teachers do ask parents to be involved, but usually when a child is having problems. They appear not to interact with them about their child's work in the ways in which Uptown teachers do. They do not get involved in developing work plans for a child who has fallen behind the rest of his or her class; instead, work is sent home, but teachers do not appear to work with parents in an active and teacherly fashion.

Lareau's description of the relation between working-class parents and schools in working-class areas is strikingly similar to ours. She characterizes it as one of separation:

> Relations between working-class families and the school are characterized by *separation*. Because these parents believe that teachers are responsible for education, they seek little information about either the curriculum or the educational process, and their criticisms of the school center almost entirely on nonacademic matters. Most working-class parents never intervene in their children's school program; their children receive a generic education. Although these parents read to their children, teach them new words, and review their papers, such activities are sporadic rather than enduring and are substantially less than what the teachers would like. (Lareau, 2000, p. 9)

Lareau attributes *separation to* the working-class parents. Our data suggests that it is a two-sided state of affairs. While clearly teachers at Downtown School did not assume nor experience the active involvement of parents that teachers of Uptown School children did, Downtown School teachers also did not engage parents in the supplementary educational work as actively as did teachers at Uptown School. Downtown School teachers seemed not to expect or look for opportunities for working with parents whose children were having problems. Sending work home with a child and having the parent check and sign it off doesn't meet the level of involvement of teachers that the Uptown teachers demonstrated. *Involvement* takes time on the part of both parents and teachers. The more classroom problems encountered by teachers, the less time they have to deal with each child and parent. So too, the less time free from employed working hours for parents, the less time they have for active involvement, whether with school or with educational work with their children.

ADMINISTRATORS

The two-sided character of the relationship between parents and the institutional responses of the school appears clearly in the ways the school administrators describe the issues for their schools. The Uptown School principal is clear about the significance of the academic background created by the kinds of middle-class parents living in the area close to the school. These are the parents whose children set the tone for the school:

> ... when you have the school where the children have good entry behavior, as we like to call it. In other words they have been

exposed to a number of areas in the academics. We find that they more or less set the tone for the school. No matter what activity you are going in, whether it be sports or representing the school in academics or in public speaking, that you have a model which the other students can follow and that this is certainly advantageous in a building when you have even 30% of your school population that have a desire and are academically oriented. That it does set that tone for the school.

Principal
Uptown School

The principal is not talking about parental involvement; he is talking about the exposure to academics. The school, as a whole, benefits from having a sufficient proportion of children with what the principal calls *good entry behavior*. As new housing developments are built in Maltby, the character of the school catchment changes, and Uptown School administrators must respond to the somewhat lower level of academic background in the children that are moving into the area. An Uptown grade 3 teacher commented on the changed character of the school community:

Maybe, I think the expectations of the Uptown School people were that their children would be achievers and they saw that they were and they were supportive. And at the same time, they would question if they felt their child had not achieved a certain level of performance. That was very important to them . . . . And I find that now if I ask the children to bring something from home or if they have any records, materials or whatever, I don't get nearly as much support that way, although the people are as interested in the children. They're very good. If you have parent-teacher night you get almost everyone here, or if you, when you're putting on a production or a concert or anything like that, the response from the community is very good. But I find that, ah, maybe the people are a little, maybe, I don't know, maybe they are more realistic. Just because you're an achiever doesn't mean that your child will be an achiever . . . and that's not necessarily true now.

This teacher speaks not only to the differences in parental resources, but also to the consequences of school program change for her classroom and the *tone of the school*:

And the gifted children have been skimmed off now. In grade 2, the gifted children have been taken up in the past couple of years and that's made a difference in the class too because I sometimes think that the rest of the children try to work up to the potential of some of the very good people in the class and some of the very good people are in other locations so, yes, I think you do have to regear your program. I'm not saying you gear it down, but you change the, your approach sometimes and maybe I'm a little more gimmicky than I was (laughter). But I think the children are as intelligent, you have to motivate a little bit more.

Grade 3 Teacher
Uptown

Indications of how a school functions became more explicit in our interviews with school administrators. At the level of the school, the issue of the kinds of parental background of the children is one of how to allocate the school resources under different conditions. The principal has to consider how to fit the children to a different grade or different levels of the same grades, and hence, how to allocate the teaching staff:

Basically, for this particular community we have found that we are, that our standardized scores for example are probably lower than what we've been accustomed to, and therefore, when we start grouping the students for instruction, we look at that. This year we just finished now our testing, just to give us a basis of what we can expect or how much growth the students can make in a year. We have found that we do have a larger number that are not making the growth rate to which we have been accustomed. Rather than having everyone at the 2 plus level, say in grade 1, we are going to have half at that level. We are going to have 15% that are showing very little growth this year. Or, I shouldn't say very little growth. The entry behavior we didn't measure, and they were new to the building. We don't know that. But where they— at the present time they are about a one four, or a one five. So we're going to have more children at that level.

Principal
Uptown

This is one area where parental involvement is not desired, at least by this principal. The allocation of children to classes is a matter, in his view, of professional judgment. Formerly, parents shopped around for teachers. But the principal has limited this practice by limiting parental visits to their own children's classrooms, and not informing parents until class allocations have already been made (without their input) at the beginning of the fall term.[1]

Downtown School teachers and the principal confront a very different community. The Downtown School principal views the school as a mixture of a core of supportive parents and others who have an uncertain interest or involvement in their children's education:

> This is a center city school. We have a number of fine parents and they are the backbone of the parent help within the school. Coupled with that, we have, I would say more than many outlying schools: couples who perhaps are both working, single parents, single fathers, couples living together, and so on. Within the area also, we have a number of hostels for children who have been through the courts, for families who have separated, the mothers come in and settle in our area and children are sent here to school. It poses a number of extra problems for staff and academic resource personnel to try and have programs for these children at their level, at their abilities.

He identifies the problems confronted by teachers as problems of attitude rather than a lack of academic background. When a child is in trouble with his or her work, parents cannot be counted on to provide supplementary educational support:

> I: Can you give me an example of an attitude?
> P: A family for example: Single parent, father is at home, mother has tried to come back because of the problems with the children. She was the steady influence in the home as far as the children were concerned. She cannot survive [in the home] because what she says is not backed up by the father. The father leaves for work maybe 7:00 in the morning and doesn't get home until 5-ish at night. I try to call at night or whenever and I can't . . . even at work I'll phone to catch him. One son has gone through and was nothing but a problem from day one, behavior-wise, lackadaisical. The father says, "Oh yes, it'll get done" but nothing is ever done at home. We used to try sending books home, the father sees that the work is done, signs the book when the work is finished, and the book is returned the next day. The book never survived more than 2 or 3 days —definitely not a week. So after

trying a number of books, we gave up on that recourse. A second son is now in grade 8 —better worker, but again no incentive of any kind. Not responsive to kindness unless it's something that he wants. For example, the father will say, "Well, I have no problems at home" and with further questioning he'll say "Well, he doesn't do that at home either" and so you keep going and finally come to the decision that the reason he has no problems is because he doesn't demand anything from the children. He doesn't confront them with what is right and what is wrong and that's one example of what I'm referring to . . . I might add that that's a low percentage in the school. But we do have a percentage, maybe in that class 5% there. If you take that 5% and split it through the school you'd end up with fifteen students. I feel that's a serious situation.

Principal
Downtown

The central office assistant superintendent, who is responsible for the area in which Downtown School is situated, describes a process by which teachers' expectations of children have adjusted downward to meet those of the parents:

Frankly, the level of expectations on the part of the parents for many of the students is the same expectations that their parents had for them. That was to graduate from high school with an education sufficient to be able to get a job. To attain a college or university degree is not seen as the highest form, but getting a job, being able to be actively employed at Big Plant or the support services in Maltby is a very good goal to have. Students, therefore, don't have tremendously high expectations. What happens is that because of these expectations, the expectations on the part of the staff have gradually lowered. There is a feeling that there are low expectations, on the part of the community, for the attainment of their children in education, so I think what has happened has been a gradual drifting down of expectations on the part of staff.

Assistant Superintendent
South Maltby

The Downtown School principal describes an institutionalizing of this downward shift as it has come to shape the educational objectives of the school:

We look at the students who come and we say, "there is no way they can learn how to cover the whole course." It's impossible. They don't even know how to do the first part of it, let alone the last. So what we are going to concentrate on are those things that can basically help them survive—how to handle money, how to be punctual and on time, and how to tell time properly, and how to do problem solving, how to do interest. They are going to be handling interest out there—interest on a car, interest on a home, how to do a bank account. Well that would be petty stuff for some of them over there [in the middle-class school]. But for here, it's life skills tied in with math that they are doing every day. They'll get the same math but not to the depth that they would get there. All right? Because number one, the students couldn't handle it here.

Principal
Downtown School

This stabilization of Downtown School's work with children at a lower level of performance than would be expected in a middle-class school is *not* simply a product of the kind of economic base described by the assistant superintendent:

[An area of] single parent families, subsidized housing, both parents working, low income, high transience rate—all of those things would be typical of the population of Downtown School. While there are many single dwellings and duplexes, there is no high rise apartments per se, but there is subsidized housing. The housing is generally of a poorer nature than it would be in North Maltby. Very work-oriented people, very task-oriented people, really working very hard to make ends meet, and meet the mortgage and food payments.

Assistant Superintendent
South Maltby

The realities of the local economy disappear in what educators conceive of as *expectations* and *attitudes*. When the responsible parent does not undertake putting home time into supplementary educational work, even if it's only overseeing a child's performance level on work that he or she has brought home, then that child is at a disadvantage. When, however, there is a significant percentage of parents who, for whatever reason, are unable to respond to the teacher's attempts to have the child supplement work in the school setting with work at home, then this is a problem not just for the individual children, but for the work of the classroom as a whole. It is consequential, as Manicom demonstrates, for how teachers must allocate their teaching time in the classroom. If having a sufficient percentage of children with good academics in their background raises the performance level of the whole school, as the Uptown principal suggests, then it is likely that the opposite effect is at work in the Downtown School setting. This effect is intensified when a parent does not have the time or interest to work with his or her child. Downtown teachers are able to respond only selectively to the 5% of children, that the Downtown School principal spoke of, who present serious problems. They appear to have neither the time, nor the encouragement, to attempt to make up for what parents are unable, or lack motivation, to do.

CONCLUSION

Manicom's (1988, 1995) studies suggest that inner-city school elementary children get less teaching time on the required curriculum than children in middle-class schools because teachers have to teach to the children's school-defined deficits. A study of high schools in Chicago has found that the inner-city schools in that city were short changed instructional time in comparison with suburban schools. In inner-city schools, "Each classroom period was, on average, 8 minutes less than those of their suburban peers" (Ferree, 1999, p. 58; 1986). Our interviews with parents suggest that families in which both parents work have less time to supplement the educational work of the school. Our interviews with teachers bring into view a similar lack of time at Downtown School for attending to the two-sided relation between families and schools. When parents, typically mothers, cannot or will not do the pedagogical and curricular work on which the school depends, schools are unable, or unwilling, to teach at the level expected in middle-class schools such as Uptown School. Typically, the parents' lack of attention to school needs is seen as a matter of parental expectations or their attitude towards their children's education. As our data shows, the two-sided relation between families and schools is predicated on family economic and educational resources, and, as Lareau (1987) reminds us, the ability of parents and children to work together on the educational project is defined by the school. Where any one of these aspects of the relation is not present, the two-sided relation on which schooling depends is abrogated and the school is unable to make up the differences.

7

INEQUALITY AND
EDUCATIONAL CHANGE

Our approach in this book has been that of institutional ethnography. Our final chapter reassembles our various discoveries, both the original research and the historical trajectory in which the book's overall perspective is located, to reconstruct the logic of the project. We have also tried to evaluate the implications of differences in economic organization for the mothering-school relation. Institutional ethnography begins in people's experience in an institutional setting. We started with our own experiences as single parents when our children were in elementary school. Then, we went on to explore the experiences of women who were members of normal families, that is, families that conformed to the traditional model of wife, husband, and children.

Experience, of course, is a method of telling stories; its content is not already discursively committed. In talking with one another, and then, in interviewing women for what became our study, we needed a discursive focus. Two or three steps away from Marx, and only very distantly connected to his concept of *labor*, we had come upon the thinking of a group called Wages for Housework. Wages for Housework had expanded the women's movement's discovery of housework as work. Theirs was a generous conception of *work* involving almost everything that people do and that is presupposed as an essential part of their employment. They included not only what was traditionally known as housework, but such activities as driving a car to work, taking clothes to the cleaners, picking up a child from school, and so on. *Work*, in this sense, means what is done intentionally under definite material conditions and taking definite amounts of time. For our first discussions, this was the concept that made observable for us what was involved in getting our children off to school so that they'd be there on time—the rush to get back from work in time to be home when the children came home, or to pick them up at the school—visits to the school to see the teacher—dealing with anxieties and fears that children from time to time brought home, and much more. As we spoke with the women in Turner's Crossing, where we had lots of conversational interview time, more and more we discovered the richness and potentiality that this concept of *work* yielded as discursive focus.

Getting cut off in our research at Turner's Crossing resulted in a radical limitation on our explorations of women's experiences. In order to get through the needed number of interviews in the time available, we had to narrow the focus of our interviews. They were still organized by the concept of *work*, but our focus was restricted more to the school day as an organizing principle; the interviews were less expansive and more structured.

Institutional ethnography doesn't stop with people's experiences. Providing an account of some of the work that women do in relation to their children's schooling is not an end in itself. Our exploration moved deeper, following the relevancies of the concerns that had come out of our own experience as single parents, to trace the institutional order as we and the women whom we interviewed participated in it. We discovered that the mothering discourse, the discourse that constitutes mothers as subjects within educational institutions, orients the work that they do and subordinates us appropriately to the authority of educational experts. After the interviewing phase of our study was completed, we came to see that the mothering discourse had become the framework within which our interviews had been conducted. Only then could we recognize that not all those mothers we talked to were participants in the discourse.

In examining further how the work being done in a particular setting of an institutional regime hooks into that regime itself, we made use of the concept of *social relation*. We use this in a way that draws on Marx. He does not use *social relation* to mean relationship, but rather to trace the coordination of people's doings in social sequences that are not necessarily visible to any individual involved, are not intentional, or managed. We took up aspects of the work that the mothers described in order to locate them in a social relation to the work of the school. First, we saw women dealing with the problem of how to coordinate the various schedules of family members so as to produce, in conjunction with the school, the orderly process of the school day. We also saw that there were variations here. Mothers whose children went to school in a largely middle-class area were all very much concerned with the punctual arrival of their children in school; mothers with children attending school in the lower-income area were more variable in their approaches. While some of the working-class mothers engaged with the school routines in ways that were not very different from middle-class mothers, there were others who seemed disinterested in issues of punctuality. Complimentarily, we found that the school in the middle-class area, Uptown School, simply took for granted in their school scheduling that children would be on time. This assumption was not present in Downtown School, where the first period of the day was set up to allow leeway so that those few children who might be late would not disrupt the order of the classroom. Our interviewing procedure had taken the school day for granted. Our interviews, with their focus on the work of getting children to school, on being available when they came home from school, and so on, showed us how the very standardization on which teaching and learning in Uptown School relied was itself being produced at this conjunction of mothers' and educators' work.

A major focus of our interviews was the work that women were doing that could be considered as complementing the educational work of the school. As we've shown, it was indeed mothers who were doing the largest part of the work involved, though the differences between mothers and fathers were perhaps more striking among those whose children attended Uptown School. Most of the mothers of children at Uptown School did not work outside the home and were available when their children came home after school to spend time with them, whereas those with children at Downtown School were more likely to be pressed for time and were less available. Our emphasis, however, in exploring the educational work done in the home, was not on the outcomes of the family's educational work for an individual child (which has been the continuing emphasis on research that examines the relationship between family and school achievement). Rather, the conceptual shift we have made addresses women's mothering work *in relation to the educational work of teachers and administrators*, creating the conditions and possibilities of teaching and learning in the school or in the school district.

The relation is two sided; the predominantly middle-class community on which Uptown School draws is one in which teachers and administrators can count on a high level of involvement from parents. It also clearly includes educational work done in the home that registers in the account of one administrator as familiarity with "academics." It doesn't have to be all the children in the school but there have to be enough to establish a school's character. Teachers can rely on, though they sometimes feel pressured by, the level of interest that parents of Uptown School children display. They draw on mothers' efforts to supplement classroom teaching. We don't know whether they are fully aware of the everyday educational work that we heard of through the women's stories, but we did hear how Uptown School teachers can pretty much take for granted that a child's mother will put in time to help the child if she or he is having difficulty.

Downtown School teachers not only have a different experience with their school population in general, but they also do not appear to look for and encourage the active participation of parents in the work of education. The problems of time and pressures of employment, as well as a clear alienation among some parents from the very project represented by the school, present themselves as general conditions for the school. Individual parents who might be looking for a different kind and level of participation in their children's schooling will not find a supporting response at the Downtown School.

The two-sided relation works from the school's side at the generalized level—this is how a school can function in a particular setting. The two-sided relation is one celebrated by the Uptown School principal, who says that it is clear that it makes a difference "when you have even 30% of your school population that have a desire and are academically oriented." We do not have a similar estimate of percentages from Downtown School, but our own small collection of interviews in this book suggests some of the differences that may exist between the communities served by the two schools. But again, we want to emphasize how the social relation becomes stabilized in an institutional form. This is not simply parental educational work. Uptown School parents and Uptown School teachers and administrators are implicated in a complementary relation in which the school educators take for granted, encourage, and rely on the work of the mothers at home. By contrast, the organization of the relations between parents, their educational work and interests in Downtown School go largely unrecognized and unsupported by teachers and administrators whose work responds less to individuals than to the actual collections of children that they must work with in the classroom every day.

We wrote about our research earlier, though the present work also offers a reworking and reanalysis of much of our data. In locating ourselves, we used the notion of a *historical trajectory* that could be traced from the revision of the middle class in the late nineteenth and early twentieth centuries and the importance of education and credentials in the organization of the new middle class into our own time. We have proposed that our own story, and the stories of women that we have knitted into an account of the differences between Uptown and Downtown Schools, are to be seen in continuity with a specialization of the work of middle-class women in relation to their children's schooling. That contributes, we argued, in major ways to the differentiation of the middle-class child's educational experience, and hence, to reproducing the kinds of advantages that the new and credentialed middle class has secured, at least until recently. A distinctive gender organization that is, as we have seen, foundational to the different educational capacities of schools in middle-class as contrasted with low-income communities, emerged and has been perpetuated.

In this book, an *engine of inequality* has been described, interlocking the unpaid labor of (middle-class) women in the home and the local practices of schools. The level of educational work possible in a school depends on the general level of background educational work contributed by the homes in the area. We can imagine an educational system that short circuits the operation of this engine. For example, a school system might extend the work of schooling to reduce or eliminate the school's reliance on educational work done in the home by making prekindergarten available to every child (Head Start was an attempt of this kind); by radically reducing class size, particularly at elementary levels so that teachers can work in conditions under which they can realistically respond to the individual child's needs; by revising curriculum and pedagogic practices to respond more realistically to the learning needs of children of all economic, racial, and ethnic groups. We began the research for this book almost 20 years ago. What we have seen since then has moved in a direction far from the public school system of our imagination.

EDUCATION AND THE CHANGING REGIME OF ACCUMULATION

A *regime of accumulation* is a concept that combines capitalism's essential process of accumulation (that is always on the move and is essentially destabilizing) with a recognition of periods of relative stability, in which institutional forms have emerged, that regulate the process. A period sometimes known as *Fordism* was coming to an end at the time of our research. Processes of restructuring and reorganization have been underway particularly since the early 1980s, in which competition and corporate forms of economic organization and production have been increasingly organized globally. The imperatives of new forms of accumulation discipline and reshape public institutions, and a new regime of accumulation has begun to emerge, involving the withdrawal of public resources from the sphere of the reproduction of people's lives, including public schooling.

The past 5 years have seen extensive and dramatic changes in the education systems of many societies including Canada, Australia, Chile, New Zealand, the U.K., the U.S., and more recently, Denmark (Bascia & Hargreaves, 2000; Griffith & Reynolds, 2002). The educational changes occurring today are one aspect of a major shift in economic organization involving an "alteration of the state's economic role, privatization, mass unemployment and the restructuring of the labor force, and the alteration of the legislative framework defining . . . the boundaries and scope of the welfare state" (Mohun, 1994, p. 552). Piece by piece, and not at all systematically, new institutional arrangements are being put in place. Ideological shifts in public discourse play an active role in engineering institutional change. In Canada, the reductions in government funding have been dramatic. In Ontario, for example, public school funding has been cut by some 12% (Axelrod, 2001, pp. 2, 8). Current educational reforms are marked by top-down, large-scale changes including the following:

> Reductions in overall state funding for education—contradictory and uneven moves to decentralize school governance while simultaneously centralizing curriculum planning and assessment procedures by tying them to fiscal controls and accounting practices—shifts from collective bargaining to individual and competitive negotiations with teachers and other educational workers about contracts, wages, and working conditions —and moves to commercialize and privatize many education services and to introduce forms of parental choice. (Dehli, 1996, pp. 364–65)

"Neoconservative discourse defines citizenship in a way which denies that the citizen can claim universal social rights from the state" (Brodie, 1994, p. 56). At this crucial juncture, in which a new regime of accumulation is becoming institutionalized, the language of public discourse will not justify expanding the responsibility of public schools to replace the unpaid educational work that women have been doing. The dominant neoconservative ideologies enjoin the individual citizen to take responsibility for herself or himself, and the family is the responsible unit

so far as its members are concerned. Increasingly, as the economic resources for schooling decline, problems with schools, schooling, and
young people are represented as the responsibility of families rather
than as calling for a retooling of public educational institutions to respond to new demands. Jonathan Kozol cites a series of Wall Street
Journal articles which assert that increasing public funding to education
has no effect:

> "Big budgets don't boost achievement," it announces in [an] ar-
> ticle. "It's parental influence that counts." "Money, in fact," the
> paper says, is "getting a bad name . . . . Indeed, our fixation on
> numbers—spending per pupil, teacher salaries, class size—may
> only be distracting us from more fundamental issues . . . . It is
> even possible to argue that schools themselves don't matter
> much, at least compared with parental influence . . . . Cash alone
> can't do the trick . . . . The U.S. has already tried that . . . It has
> failed . . . ." (Wall Street Journal editorial, 1990, cited in Kozol,
> 1991, p. 134)

Neoconservative ideology provides no foothold for arguing that schools
should aim at creating greater equity among people. Relegating the responsibility for children to families assumes that parents can always im-
plement the educational best for their children.

The decline of the traditional male-headed family is represented as
eroding the moral basis of the society (Eyer, 1996). Charles Murray
(1990), an American sociologist, argues that the emergence and spread
of under-classes in the United States and Britain has nothing to do with
economic conditions, such as the globalization of industrial production, but is due to the moral failure of mothers. Thus, issues of poverty
become redefined as moral problems (Polokaw, 1993): the defective,
female-headed family, is represented as both symptom and cause even
by such critical writers as William Julius Wilson (1987). In emphasizing
the importance of economic deprivations for the black family, Wilson
focuses exclusively upon the issue of jobs for black men, and replicates
stereotypes of the moral ill effects of the mother-headed black family
(Smith, 1992). In the absence of the everyday practical welding of
masculine authority in the family to the conditions of wage earning,
contemporary men's movements seek a new commitment to making
the traditional idealization a design for living. Tony Evans, a leader
in the Promise Keepers movement (a men's movement), urges men to
take back their leadership of the family whether their wives consent

or not, and women to give back leadership to their husbands "for the sake of . . . our culture" (Minkowitz, 1995, p. 69). The moral preeminence of the new familism being established in public discourse reshapes institutions to support the privatization of formerly public functions in the new regime of accumulation.

CHANGING FAMILY ORGANIZATION

The economic bases of family organization have been transformed in the last 20 years. In general, the time available to all families, including families in the middle classes, to complement the educational work of the school has been significantly reduced. Juliet Schor (1992) has described the increasing demands on the employed time of both women and men: At the beginning of the 1990s, men were working outside the home on average an additional 100 hours per year, that is, 2 and $^1/_2$ weeks. The increases in women's work hours were even more dramatic. Their working hours in employment had increased by 300 hours per year, an additional 7 and $^1/_2$ weeks per year. Households became increasingly dependent on the earnings of both wives and husbands. In 1994, a study by the US Department of Education expressed concerns about the lack of time available for parents to be actively involved in their children's education. The labor force involvement of married women had increased significantly.

> [I]n 1996 [in the U.S.], 76.7% of married mothers, 80.6% of divorced or widowed mothers, and 71.8% of never-married mothers with school age children were in the labor force. (Crawford and Levitt, 1999)

In Canada, in the same year 69.1% of married mothers with children under 6, and 78.6% of married mothers with children between 6–14 were employed (Vanier Institute of the Family, 2002).

Such changes in the economic bases of the family household means that many parents are experiencing conditions and constraints that deprive them of the resources, particularly of time, that parents can contribute to the work of educators in the schools attended by their children. The availability of parents, and particularly of mothers, to do this unpaid educational work is assumed in the standardized organization and curriculum of elementary schools. Manicom's (1988, 1995) studies have identified just those differences in the teacher's work that the presence or absence of mothers' complementary educational work makes in the classroom. We have heard also, from the school adminis-trators in Maltby, of the sensitivity of a school operation to changes in the demographics of a given area. Where parent educational work is unavailable in the communities they serve, schools must operate at a lower level of educational effectiveness. Changes in family organization have changed the kind and level of work teachers and administrators are able to do at the same time that widespread reductions in staffing has reduced their ability to respond (Levin, 2000). There is no provision for extending school responsibility into the areas that parents are unable to sustain, and under contemporary ideological conditions, there is no public discourse that impels such expansion. A public discourse laying responsibility on the family justifies a public educational system that in-tensifies inequalities, if only by concealing the economic conditions that underlie the improvising of a new and more radically differentiating en-gine of inequality. It is a discourse that excludes, from the currency of public discourse, the concept of a society's interest in the education of our children, or of democracy's need for an educated citizenry. Reassembled or retooled, the pieces of the old engine of inequality pull parents who have time, resources, and skills into intensifying their un-paid labor to supplement the work of schooling.

The general changes sketched above do not register the kinds of changes in numbers of children growing up in poverty. In a 1995 inter-national comparison of relative rates of child poverty in eighteen in-dustrialized countries, the United States had the highest rates, with one in five children living in poverty; Canada was not far behind, with ap-proximately one in ten. A 1998–2000 National Population Health Survey "revealed that Canadian children under 17 were the age group most likely to live in food-insecure households where there isn't enough money to buy sufficient food or the right kinds of food" (Canadian Council on Social Development, 2002). In the United States in particu-lar, the introduction of the Personal Responsibility and Work Oppor-tunities Reconciliation Act in 1996 has meant that people, particularly sole-support mothers, who would in the past have been entitled to wel-fare, are now required to enter the labor force.

Similar changes have been introduced in Canada. Wherever they are introduced, they have hidden implications for what happens to the chil-dren of such families. Elizabeth Higginbotham's (2001) study of black women who have been to college or university describes how the mother of one of those she interviewed managed on welfare. Mrs. Washington "combined community work with child rearing" and "used the means within her reach to encourage her children in academic pursuits." Their home was full of books and records. Contemporary conditions preclude such possibilities and opportunities for mothers living in poverty and hence for their children.

Perhaps our study had too narrow a conception of what is involved in doing mothering work under contemporary conditions of poverty. We focused too exclusively on labor force participation, a further indication of how the mothering discourse pervaded our thinking in the earlier stages of our study. We did not consider such matters as access to libraries, to transportation, to health care.

Perhaps if we had had a chance to pursue the style of interviewing that characterized our exploration of their work with mothers in Turner's Crossing, we would have learned a great deal more about other conditions that are associated with living in a predominantly low-income area. A passage from an interview done by Michele Fine, in her evaluation of three parental involvement projects in the United States, brings into view other conditions of mother's work we did not even begin to think about. Take the following account from one interview for example:

> You see, I work 10 hours a day, and I can't be, cause, society blames it on the parents a lot. And I think, I think that I'm a good parent. I don't take drugs, I drink occasionally, but I don't do drugs, I don't have drugs in my house and so it's not something he's seen me, he hasn't seen me sell drugs, so I don't know what he does, but then society says well, you're supposed to know what your children doing at all times. It's not so. I take 2 hours to travel to work, 2 hours to travel back, and I'm on my feet 10 hours a day. So, that's like 14 hours a day, I'm out of the house. (Fine, 1993, p. 687)

Where there are no controls over hours of work, where public transportation is inadequate, where the neighborhood itself creates special problems for parental control and supervision of their children, the availability of parents to put time into direct involvement with the school is clearly going to be radically limited.

Rather than mobilizing the school system to respond to these changed situations, the strategies of reducing public expenditures in the public sphere has gone in precisely the opposite direction. Increasing class size and dwindling personnel and library resources decreases a school's ability to meet the share of educational work to which it had formerly been committed. A *Globe and Mail* article notes the following:

[The new curricular standards are part of] a system at odds with itself. When the curriculum was introduced, the Progressive Conservative government also decreed that teachers receive fewer training days, rather than more. At the same time, the government gave teachers more classes to teach, cutting their preparation time. And budget cuts meant fewer remedial supports. (November 29, 2001, p. A25)

Teachers have less time to individuate their teaching for children who, for whatever reason, and sometimes for only transitory periods, need extra attention to bring them up to the level of the rest of the class. Larger classes also often mean more heterogeneity, thus compounding the problem of keeping everyone up to speed. The work of teaching, in itself, has changed while teachers must handle larger numbers with fewer and less diverse resources.

CONCLUSION

The study by Fine (2001) referred to above provides a mixed picture of various attempts to take up the concept of parental involvement as a practical solution to the problems of schools. Our study has been oriented rather differently. We have been exploring how the public school system, with its apparent potential for equity, has been hijacked, largely by middle-class women, to become *an engine of inequality*. Changes in the last 20 years have removed many of the economic underpinnings of the middle-class family household that originated in the late nineteenth and early twentieth centuries. Despite the longer hours of paid employment and the increased dependence of families on two earners, middle-class parents are somehow finding time to play an active part in their children's schooling. An article in the *Toronto Star* is headed: "Parents prop up schools. Volunteer work, fund raising hide full effects of education cuts, critics say." (April 8, 2000, p. J1). The article also describes parents teaching music and art in some primary schools.

The present situation, while dismantling the earlier securities of middle-class advantages in the public school situation, is intensifying the educational and related work, as well as the stress of middle-class parenting. Furthermore, it has not fundamentally changed the systematic production of inequality that our study has explored. The historical continuity is indicated in Alison's recent interviews (in early April 2001 and in February 2002) with two middle-class mothers.

Both mothers are involved in education; both have boys who were 11 at the time of these interviews. Sarah's son is in public school in Canada. Nancy's son is in a private school in Louisiana. Sarah's son is struggling with the new Ontario curriculum. Nancy's son maintains good grades in relation to the nationalized curriculum of the private school. Both Sarah and Nancy have more-than-adequate educational, social, and economic resources to support their children's schooling. They also have flexible work schedules that allow them to reschedule work appointments if they are required to attend an event or meeting at the school. Both mothers tell of long hours helping their sons with their homework.

For Nancy, helping means monitoring her son's school progress by reviewing the schoolwork he brings home, working intensively with him to ensure that his homework is not only complete but done accurately and neatly, reading his textbooks on the topics with which she does not feel comfortable so that she can work with him on his school assignments, instructing him on how to do library and internet research, and so on. Nancy claims that if she didn't spend 2 to 4 hours per night (including weekends) working with John, he would not be able to keep his grades up, and therefore, jeopardize his entrance into a good university.

For Sarah, helping means working with her son on his homework every evening and at least once during the weekend. Ira receives passing grades on most of his academic work and good grades in Music and Art —two areas of the curriculum that have been cut back by the current Ontario government. Ira is not enthusiastic about school, and often avoids school assignments by not telling his mother what he has to do. At times, when Sarah and Ira work on his homework, both become very upset and much of the homework time is spent trying to find a way to resolve the emotional difficulties that arise (see also Lareau, 1996). Because of the difficulty that they have working together, Sarah has hired a tutor who works with Ira after Saturday Hebrew school. This combination of support has allowed Ira to maintain his passing grades.

These two mothers are very well educated and their children attend schools that are able to maintain a strong family-school relationship. Substantively, their mothering work has not changed from that of mothers with children in schools in the late 1980s and early 1990s, or indeed from the time when Dorothy and Alison were mothers with children in school. What has changed is the *amount* of work demanded by the school in order for their students to progress through the graded curriculum. Both mothers spend many hours supervising, helping, and working with their children on homework. Educational restructuring includes less money for teaching resources. In Ontario, it has also included more difficult topics taught at an earlier age and higher curricular standards. The work required to fill the gap between higher standards and fewer resources is mothering, and sometimes fathering, work.

But this handoff of schoolwork to the family is not evenly spread across all schools. In contrast to the school demands on mothering work described above, Robert's sons attend a working-class school in British Columbia. The oldest son, Jeremy, is 13 and on the Honor Roll. In primary school, a teacher told him that very few of his classmates would go to a university and asked him to promise that he would. The youngest son, Tim, is 11 and has had difficulty learning to read. Robert and Anna have been to the school several times to discuss Tim's reading problems, but the school has done little in response. Jeremy averages between 1 and 3 hours of homework each night. On most nights, Tim has 15 to 45 minutes of assigned homework. Both boys love to play games on the Internet, and Robert and Anna have had to limit computer time.

The differences between the families', and between the three schools' demands for parental support are striking:

- The private school in Louisiana claims that 98% of their students attend university after graduation. Their curriculum is oriented to a set of national standards that do not originate in Louisiana, but rather, are focused on top-ranked university entrance. Families whose children attend the school have, or have access to, economic and social resources that will support their educational work.
- The Ontario public school is situated in a middle-class neighborhood. Many of the parents have higher education degrees and they pressure the school to meet the new curricular standards, even when they may not agree with them. The new Ontario curriculum is matched by standardized testing that identifies the students' level of learning and compares test scores across schools. Implicitly, these scores also test teachers and principals who are under growing pressure to show that their school scores are increasing.
- The school in British Columbia enrolls a range of children; some are from families who have recently immigrated to Canada; some are from families whose income is below the poverty line; some are from middle-income families. The teachers' low expectations of their students are considered to be realistic, given their family backgrounds.

In these stories, we can identify the survival of the institutional forms of the family–school relation that formed what we called the *engine of inequality*. They have been significantly modified, at least in the case of the middle-class mothers, by the changed economic and social conditions in which schools and families now operate. Though they may make the educational contribution of middle-class parents more strenuous and demanding, the new policies and educational reforms do nothing to change the family–schooling relation described in this book and the ways in which it reproduces, and may indeed enhance, social inequality.

Endnotes

Introduction

1. The research and writing for this book was funded, in part, by a grant from the Social Science and Humanities Research Council (410-84-0450), the Spencer Foundation (Minigrant, 1992), Faculty of Education Minor Research Grants, and an SSHRC Small Research Grant, York University.
2. The phrase *relations of ruling* designates the complex of extralocal relations that provide in contemporary societies a specialization of organization, control and initiative (Smith, 1990, p. 6). The relations of ruling are primarily textually mediated communicative practices.
3. At the time of our study, Turner's Crossing and Maltby were almost exclusively white, although both cities had diverse ethnic populations. Only one mother was a first-generation immigrant. While the neighborhoods in which we interviewed have stayed essentially the same, the suburbs surrounding these cities have grown dramatically over the past 20 years and are multilingual, multicultural, and multiracial. The implications of these demographic changes will be addressed in further research.
4. The superintendent at the time felt that our proposed engagement with schools attended by the children of the women we'd talked to would be disruptive, and the board refused us permission to interview their teachers and principals. Access would be denied. We had no option but to start all over again. In keeping with interviewing ethics, names of cities here are pseudonyms.
5. At least north of the border with Mexico.

Chapter 1

1. Poulantzas (1975) distinguishes those new petty bourgeoisies who work under conditions most comparable to those of the working class as doing "nonproductive labor."
2. Other Marxist theorists tend to adopt theoretical strategies that reduce the changes we are attending to the binary of capitalist and worker; Marxist theorizing is resistant to moving away from a binary class structure of capitalists confronting a working class, for example, "to the highest level of abstraction—that of the pure capitalist mode of production—only two classes need to be considered: the capitalist class and the working class. . . ." In concrete analyses, however, new positions emerge, but these are viewed "as intervening locations between polarized classes" (Clegg, Boreham, & Dove, 1986, p. 144). Erik Olin Wright (1985) resolves the salaried middle class into "contradictory

class locations" in his theorizing of class in contemporary American society.

3. Though analogous developments have also been taking place in Europe, both in the capitalist west and the socialist east, North American developments have distinctive social organizational features and it is aspects of these on which we focus.

4. It had earlier existed largely as a means through which state functions were farmed out to private enterprise (Roy, 1997).

5. Though Davidoff and Hall's major study of the emergence of the forms of family and gender among the middle classes is of England, we cite it here because of their admirable account of the intermixing of business and family life. See in particular their chapter on "The Hidden Investment: Women and the Enterprise."

6. Marisol Pérez-Lizaur (1997) has drawn a fascinating picture of the family enterprise in Mexico and its encounter with the radically new forms of organization characteristic of the contemporary international market. Dorinne Kondos' (1982) account of her experience working for a family enterprise in Japan provides another viewpoint on the same encounter, written from the perspective of workers who were not family members.

7. With the encouragement of northern foundations such as the Ford Foundation, and in opposition to notable African American intellectuals such as W. E. B. DuBois, the schools and colleges of the southern United States in particular emphasized vocational education in secondary and postsecondary institutions (Turner, 1990; Collins, 1979, p. 115).

8. The child in the literature on child rearing that we read was implicitly male.

9. Walkerdine (1984) brings into view the discursive links between education and psychology that shape our knowledge of children's maturation.

10. Miriam David (1980, 1993) has written of the British version of this contradiction. She argues that schooling is implicated in the ongoing inequality of women and is an integral part of the family-school nexus.

Chapter 2

1. See Griffith (1984) for an analysis of the concept of *single parent* as constituent of an educational discourse with multiple sites—administration, school, newspapers, social service agencies, and so forth.

2. Chamboredon and Prevot (1975) describe analogous developments in France linking the normative child development paradigm and home-school based pedagogy. The conception of childhood as developmentally distinct stages stipulates stage-specific educational practices. The designation of the years between two and five as *early childhood*, a crucial period in the child's development, constructed the child as the focus of mothering and teaching practices, making the child the pedagogical subject of her mother's educational work in the French bourgeois home. Chamboredon and Prevot's analysis illustrates the relationship between the conceptions of children's maturation held within the child development discourse and the complementary, but invisible, mothering work on which it depends.

Chapter 3

1. Notice the term *stability* here. It's a term that betrays the organizing presence of the mothering discourse.

2. In the following chapter, we take up the after school time as a key period in the day for the educational work of parents.

Chapter 4

1. In her dissertation, Manicom elaborates on these notions of *readiness*, *normal pace*, and *mandated curriculum*.
2. We will explore fathers' work more fully in the next chapter.

Chapter 5

1. Our data doesn't allow more confidence in this statement since we did not ask about reading separately from other kinds of supplementary educational work.
2. In addition to Bill Ames's active involvement, Helen Moore reports that her husband helps her older son, now 12, with his assignments; both Bill and Wayne are Uptown School fathers.
3. The bracket around Orton's name locates her exceptionality as someone who is in a position to purchase others' time to substitute for her own long hours at work to supplement her own commitment to "mothering as teaching."

Chapter 6

1. Here is one example of the change in educational practice between the time of our research and now. Currently, parents are encouraged to participate in the school administration through the School Advisory Council, as well as informally in ways that this principal would discourage. We will come back to this issue in chapter 8.

Bibliography

Abbott, P., & Wallace, C. (1992). *The family and the new right*. London: Pluto Press.

Acker, J. (1980). Women and stratification: A review of recent literature. *Contemporary Sociology, 9,* 25–39.

Althusser, L. (1971). Ideology and ideological state apparatuses. In B. Brewster (Trans.), *Lenin and Philosophy and Other Essays*. New York: Monthly Review Press.

Andre-Becheley, L. (2004). The goals of a voluntary integration program and the problems of access: A closer look at a magnet school application procedure. *Equity and Excellence in Education*, Special Issue: *Brown v. Board of Education* + 50, 37 (3). 302–315.

Andre-Becheley, L. (2005). Public school choice at the intersection of voluntary integration and not-so-good neighborhood schools: Lessons from parent's experiences. *Educational Administration Quarterly*, 41 (2). Forthcoming.

Apple, M.W. (2000). *Official knowledge* (2nd ed.). New York: Routledge.

Apple, M.W. (2001). *Educating the "right" way: Markets, standards, God, and inequality*. New York: RoutledgeFalmer.

Apple, M.W., et al. (2003). *The state and the politics of knowledge*. New York: RoutledgeFalmer.

Armstrong, P., & Armstrong, H. (1983). Beyond sexless class and classless sex: Towards Feminist Marxism. *Studies in Political Economy, 10,* Winter 7–44.

Arnup, K. (1994). *Education for motherhood: Advice for mothers in twentieth-century Canada*. Toronto: University of Toronto Press.

Axelrod, P. (2001). Neo-conservatism and the politics of Ontario education. *Our Schools/Ourselves, 10* (2), 51–72.

Bagdikian, B. (1992). *The media monopoly* (4th ed.). Boston: Beacon Press.

Bakhtin, M. M. (1986). *Speech genres and other late essays*. Austin: University of Texas Press.

Ball, S. (2003). *Class strategies and the education market*. London: RoutledgeFalmer.

Bascia, N., & Hargreaves, A. (2000). *The sharp edge of educational change: Teaching, leading and the realities of reform*. London & New York: Routledge.

Beck, R. H. (1965). *A social history of education*. Foundations of Education Series. Englewood Cliffs, NJ: Prentice-Hall.

Beniger, J. R. (1986). *The control revolution: Technological and economic origin of the information society*. Cambridge, MA: Harvard University Press.

Berk, S. F. (Ed.). (1982). *Never done: A history of American housework*. New York: Pantheon.

Blumenthal, S. (1986). *The rise of the counter-establishment: From conservative ideology to political power*. New York: Times Books.

Bourdieu, P. (1984). *Distinction*. Cambridge, MA: Harvard University Press.

Bourdieu, P., & Passeron, J.C. (1977). *Reproduction in education, society and culture*. Beverly Hills: Sage.

Bowles, S., & Gintis, H. (1976). *Schooling in capitalist America.* New York: Basic Books.

Brodie, J. (1994). Shifting the boundaries: Gender and the politics of restructuring. In I. Bakker (Ed.), *The strategic silence: Gender and economic policy.* London: Zed Books & Ottawa: North-South Institute.

Campbell, B. (1995). Old fogeys and angry young men. *Soundings: A Journal of Politics and Culture, 1,* Autumn 47–64.

Canadian Council on Social Development. (2002). *The progress of Canada's children 2002.* Retrieved January, 2003, from http://www.ccsd.ca.

Chamboredon, J. C., & Prevot, J. (1975). Changes in the social definition of early childhood and the new forms of symbolic violence. *Theory and Society, 2*(3), 331–50.

Chandler, A. Jr. (1977). *The visible hand: The managerial revolution in American business.* Cambridge, MA: Harvard University Press.

Chavkin, N. F. (Ed.). (1993). *Families and schools in a pluralistic society.* Albany: State University of New York Press.

Chodorow, N. (1974). *The reproduction of mothering.* Berkeley: University of California Press.

Clegg, S., Boreham, P., & Dow, G. (1986). *Class, politics and the economy.* London: Routledge & Kegan Paul.

Cohen, E. G. (1965). Parental factors in educational mobility. *Sociology of Education 38*(5), 404–25.

Coleman, J. S., with Campbell, E. Q., Hobson, C. J., McPartland, J., Mood, A., Weinfeld, F. D. & York, R. L. (1966). *Equality of educational opportunity.* Washington D.C.: U.S. Government Printing Office.

Collins, R. (1979). *The credential society: An historical sociology of education and stratification.* New York: Academic Press.

Comer, J. (1986). Parent participation in the schools. *Phi Delta Kappan, 67*(6), 442–6.

———. (1988). Educating poor minority children. *Scientific American, 259*(5), 42–8.

Connell, R. W., Ashenden, D. J., Kessler, S., & Dowsett, G. W. (1982). *Making the difference.* Boston: Allen & Unwin.

Craft, M. (1970). Family, class and education: Changing perspectives. In M. Craft (Ed.), *Family, Class and Education: A Reader.* London: Longman.

Crawford, S., & Levitt, P. (1999). Social change and civic engagement: The case of the PTA. In T. Skocpol & M. P. Civic (Eds.), *Civic engagement in American democracy.* Washington, D.C. Brookings Institute Press, & New York, Russell Sage Foundation.

Cullingford, C. (1996). The role of parents in the education system. In C. Cullingford (Ed.), *Parents, education and the state.* Aldershot, Hants, UK: Arena.

Curtis, B. (1992). *True government by choice men? Inspection, education and state formation in Canada west.* Toronto. University of Toronto Press.

Cutler, W. W. III. (2000). *Parents and schools: The 150-year struggle for control in American education.* Chicago: University of Chicago Press.

Darville, R. (1995). Literacy, experience, power. In M. Campbell & A. Manicom (Eds.), *Knowledge, experience, and ruling relations: Studies in the social organization of knowledge.* Toronto: University of Toronto Press.

Dauber, S., & Epstein, J. (1993). Parents' attitudes and practices of involvement in inner-city elementary and middle schools. In N. F. Chavkin (Ed.), *Families and schools in a pluralistic society.* New York: SUNY Press.

David, M. E. (1980). *The state, the family and education.* London: Routledge & Kegan Paul.

———. (1993). *Mothers and education, inside out? Exploring family-education policy and experience.* New York: St. Martin's Press.

Davidoff, L., & Hall, C. (1987). *Family fortunes: Men and women of the English middle class, 1780–1850.* Chicago: University of Chicago Press.

Davin, A. (1978). Imperialism and motherhood. *History Workshop Journal, 5,* 9–65.

———. (1982). Child labour, the working class family and domestic ideology in 19th century Britain. *Development and Change, 13,* 633–52.

Dehli, K. (1988). *Women and class, the social organization of mothers' relations to schools in Toronto 1915–1940.* Unpublished PhD dissertation, University of Toronto.

———. (1996). Travelling tales: education reform and parental "choice" in postmodern times. *Journal of Education Policy, 11*(1), 75–88.

Dickson, M. (1988). Slipping the bonds: A narrative inquiry of women elementary educators in leadership roles. Unpublished manuscript.

Donzelot, J. (1979). *The policing of families.* New York: Pantheon.

Douglas, J. W. B. (1964). *The home and the school.* London: MacGibbon & Kee.

Ehrenreich, B., & Ehrenreich, J. (1977). The new left: A case study in professional-managerial class radicalism. *Radical America. 2*(2), 7–22.

Ehrenreich, B., & English, D. (1979). *For her own good: 150 years of the experts' advice to women.* New York: Doubleday.

Ellman, M. (1968). *Thinking about women.* New York: Harcourt Brace Jovanovich.

Elson, D. (1994). Micro, meso, macro: Gender and economic analysis in the context of policy reform. In I. Bakker (Ed.), *The strategic silence: Gender and economic policy.* London: Zed Press & Ottawa: North-South Institute.

Epstein, J. L. (1987). Parent involvement: What research says to administrators. *Education and Urban Society, 19*(2), 119–36.

———. (1996). Improving school–family–community partnerships in the middle grades. *Middle School Journal, 28*(2), 43–48.

———. (1996). New connections for sociology and education: Contributing to school reform. *Sociology of Education,* extra issue, 6–23.

Epstein, J. L., & Sanders, M. G. (1998). What we learn from international studies of school-family-community partnerships. *Childhood Education, 74*(6), 392–94.

Eyer, D. E. (1996). *Mother-infant bonding: A scientific fiction.* New Haven, CT: Yale University Press.

———. (1996). *Motherguilt: How our culture blames mothers for what's wrong with society.* New York: Times Books & Random House.

Ferree, M. M., Lorber, J., & Hess, B. B. (1999). *Revisioning gender.* Thousand Oaks, CA: Sage.

Fine, M. (1993). [Ap]parent involvement: Reflections on parents, power, and urban public schools. *Teachers College Record, 94*(4), 682–710.

Floud, J. (1961). Social class factors in educational achievement. In A. H. Halsey (Ed.), *Ability and educational opportunity.* Paris: O.E.C.D.

Foner, E. (1998). *The story of American freedom.* New York: Norton.

Foucault, M. (1979). *Discipline and punish: The birth of the prison* (A. Sheridan, Trans.). New York: Random House.

———. (1981). The order of discourse. In R. Young (Ed.), *Untying the text: A poststructuralist reader.* London: Routledge.

Fox, B. (Ed.). (1980). *Hidden in the household: Women's domestic labour under capitalism.* Toronto: The Women's Press.

Gardiner, J. (1975). The role of domestic labour. *New Left Review, 89,* 47–59.

Golden, A. (1979). *The future of intellectuals and the rise of the new class.* New York: Seabury.

Government of Ontario, Ministry of Education (1975). *Education in the primary and junior divisions: P1J1.* Toronto: Queen's Printer.

Grant, J. (1998). *Raising baby by the book.* New Haven, CT: Yale University Press.

Griffith, A. (1984). *Ideology, education, and single parent families: The normative ordering of families through schooling.* Unpublished PhD dissertation, University of Toronto.

———. (1986). Reporting the facts: Media accounts of single parent families. *Resources for Feminist Research, 15*(1), 32–43.

———. (1995). Mothering, schooling and children's development. In M. Campbell & A. Manicom (Eds.), *Knowledge, experience, and ruling relations: Studies in the social organization of knowledge.* Toronto: University of Toronto Press.

———. (October 1998). Insider/outsider: Epistemological privilege and mothering work. *Human Studies, 21*(4), 361–376.

Griffith, A., & Reynolds, C. (2002). Canadian trends in education reform. In C. Reynolds & A. Griffith (Eds.), *Equity and globalization in education*. Calgary: Detselig, pp. 239–260.

Griffith, A., & Smith, D. E. (1987). Constructing cultural knowledge: Mothering as discourse. In J. Gaskell & A. McLaren (Eds.), *Women and education: A Canadian perspective*. Calgary: Detselig.

———. (1990). What did you do in school today?: Mothering, schooling and social class. In G. Miller & J. Holstein (Eds.), *Perspectives on social problems*. Greenwich, CT: JAI.

Gruber, H. E., & Vonèche, J. J. (Eds.). (1977). *The essential Piaget*. New York: Basic.

Gubrium, J. F. (1985). Family rhetoric as social order. *Journal of Family Issues, 6*(1), 129–52.

Gubrium, J. F., & Holstein, J. A. (1987). *Experiential location and method in family studies*. Papers in family studies. Institute for Family Studies, Milwaukee, WI: Marquette University.

Gullestad, M. (1984). *Kitchen-table society: A case study of family life and friendships among young working-class mothers in urban Norway*. Oslo: Universitetsforlaget.

Habermas, J. (1989). *The structural transformation of the public sphere: An inquiry into a category of bourgeois society*. Cambridge, MA: MIT Press.

Hacker, S. (1990). *Doing it the hard way: Investigations of gender and technology*. Boston: Unwin Hyman.

Hareven, T. K. (1982). *Family time and industrial time*. London: Cambridge University Press.

Henderson, A. (1987). *The evidence continues to grow: Parents' involvement improves student achievement*. Columbia, MD: National Committee for Citizens in Education.

Henry, M. (1996). *Parent–school collaboration: Feminist organizational structures and school leadership*. Albany, NY: SUNY Press.

Hess, G. A. J. (1999). Using ethnography to influence public policy. In J. J. Schensul & M. D. LeCompte (Eds.), *Using ethnographic data: Interventions, public programming and public policy*. Walnut Creek, CA: Altamira.

Higginbotham, E. (1985). *Employment for professional black women in the twentieth century*. Memphis: Center for Research on Women.

———. (2001). *Too much to ask: Black women in the era of integration,* Chapel Hill: University of North Carolina Press.

Himmelweit, S., & Mohun, S. (1977). Domestic labour and capital. *Cambridge Journal of Economics, 1,* 15–31.

hooks, b. (1989). *Talking back: Thinking feminist; Thinking black*. Boston: South End Press.

Hrabowski F. A., Maton, K. I., & Grief, G. L. (1998). *Beating the odds: Raising academically successful African American males*. New York: Oxford University Press.

Jackson, N. S. (1982). *Stress on schools + Stress on families = Distress for children*. Ottawa: Canadian Teachers' Federation.

Jary, D., & Jary, J. (1991). *Collins dictionary of sociology*. Glasgow: Harper Collins.

Kanter, R. M. (1977). *Men and Women of the Corporation*. New York: Basic Books.

Kenway, J. (1990). Education and the right's discursive politics: Private versus state schooling. In S. J. Ball (Ed.), *Foucault and education: Disciplines and knowledge*. London: Routledge.

Kerbow, D., & Bernhardt, A. (1993). Parental intervention in the school: The context of minority involvement. In B. Schneider & J. S. Coleman (Eds.), *Parents, their children, and schools*. Boulder, CO: Westview.

Kocka, J. (1980). *White collar workers in America, 1890–1940: A social-political history in international perspective*. London & Beverly Hills: Sage.

Kondo, D. K. (1990). *Crafting selves: Power, gender and discourses of identity in a Japanese workplace*. Chicago: University of Chicago Press.

Kozol, J. (1991). *Savage Inequalities: Children in America's schools*. New York: Crow.

Ladd-Taylor, M. (1997). When the birds have flown the nest, the mother-work may still go on. In R. D. Apple & J. Golden (Eds.), *Mothers and motherhood: Readings in American history*. Columbus: Ohio State University.

Lamont, M., & Lareau, A. (1988). Cultural capital: Allusions, gaps and glissandos in recent theoretical developments. *Sociological Theory, 6*(2), 153–68.

Lareau, A. (1987). Social class and family–school relationships: The importance of cultural capital. *Sociology of Education, 60*(2), 73–85

———. (1989). *Home advantage: Social class and parental intervention in elementary education.* London & New York: Falmer Press.

———. (1994). Parent involvement in schooling: A dissenting view. In C. Fagnano & B. Weber (Eds.), *School, family and community interaction.* Boulder CO: Westview.

———. (2000). Social class and the daily lives of children. *Childhood, 7* (2), May, 155–172.

———. (2003). *Unequal childhoods: Class, race, and family life.* Berkeley: University of California Press.

Lareau, A., & Horvat, E. M. (1999). Moments of social inclusion and exclusion: Race, class and cultural capital in family–school relationships. *Sociology of Education, 72*(1), 37–53.

Lareau, A., & Shumar, W. (1996). The problem of individualism in family–school policies. *Sociology of Education,* extra issue, 24–39.

Larson, M. S. (1977). *The rise of professionalism: A sociological analysis.* Berkeley: University of California Press.

Lawrence, A. (May 7, 2002). Bad mothering moments. *The Globe and Mail,* A24.

Lewis, J. (1980). *The politics of motherhood.* London: Croom Helm.

Lidz, T., Cornelison, A., Fleck, S. & Terry, D. (1957). The intra-familial environment of schizophrenic patients. *American Journal of Psychiatry, 114,* 245.

Lightfoot, S. L. (1978). *Worlds apart.* New York: Basic.

Lipman, P. (2004). *High stakes education.* New York: RoutledgeFalmer.

Luxton, M. (1980). *More than a labour of love: Three generations of women's work in the home.* Toronto: The Women's Press.

Lynd, R. S., & Lynd, H. M. (1956). *Middletown: A study in modern American culture.* New York: Harvest.

———. (1937). *Middletown in transition: A study in cultural conflicts.* New York: Harcourt, Brace & Co.

Macdonnell, D. (1986). *Theories of discourse: An introduction.* Oxford: Basil Blackwell.

Manicom, A. (1981, October). *The reproduction of class: The relations between two work processes.* Paper presented at the Symposium on the Political Economy of Gender in Education, Ontario Institute for Studies in Education.

——— (1988). *Constituting class relations: The social organization of teachers' work.* Unpublished PhD dissertation. Faculty of Education, University of Toronto.

——— (1995). What's health got to do with it: Class, gender, and teacher's work. In M. Campbell & A. Manicom (Eds.), *Knowledge, experience, and ruling relations: Studies in the social organization of knowledge.* Toronto: University of Toronto Press.

Marx, K., & Engels, F. (1976). *The German ideology.* Moscow: Progress.

McChesney, R. W. (1997). *Corporate media and the threat to democracy.* New York: Seven Stories Press.

Mechling, J. (1975–6). Advice to historians on advice to mothers. *Journal of Social History, 2,* 46–63.

Mehan, H. (1979). *Learning lessons: Social organization in the classroom.* Cambridge, MA: Harvard University Press.

Messer-Davidow, E. (Fall 1993). Manufacturing the liberal attack on liberalized education. *Social Text, 36,* 40–79.

Miller, G. (1986). *Producing family problems: Family rhetoric and the therapeutic process.* Papers in family studies. Milwaukee, WI: Institute for Family Studies, Marquette University.

Mills, C. Wright. (1951). *White collar: The American middle classes.* London & New York: Oxford University Press.

Minkowitz, D. (November-December 1995). In the name of the father. *MS*, *6*(3), 64–71.

Mishler, E. G. (1986). *Research interviewing: Context and narrative*. Cambridge, MA, & London: Harvard University Press.

Mohun, S. (1994). Regulation. In W. Outhwaite & T. Bottomore, with E. Gellner, R. Nisbet, & A. Touraine (Eds.), *The Blackwell dicionary of twentieth century social thought*. Oxford: Blackwell.

Muller, C., & Kerbow, D. (1993). Parent involvement in the home, school and community. In B. Schneider & J. S. Coleman (Eds.), *Parents, their children and schools*. Boulder, CO: Westview.

Murray, C. (1990). *The emerging British underclass*. London: Institute of Economic Affairs.

Noble, D. (1979). *America by design: Science, technology and the rise of corporate capitalism*. Oxford: Oxford University Press.

Noble, J. (1982). Developing the child. Unpublished manuscript. Department of Sociology, University of Toronto.

Oakes, J. (1985). *Keeping track*. New Haven, CT: Yale University Press.

Oakley, A. (1974). *The sociology of housework*. Toronto: Random House.

Pérez-Lizaur, M. (1997). The Mexican family enterprise faces the open market. *Organization: The Interdisciplinary Journal of Organization, Theory and Society*, *4*(4), 535–51.

Phillips, J. L. (1969). *The origins of intellect: Piaget's theory*. San Francisco: W.H. Freeman.

Polokaw, V. (1993). *Lives on the edge: Single mothers and their children in the other America*. Chicago: University of Chicago Press.

Poulantzas, N. (1975). *Classes in contemporary capitalism*. London: New Left Books.

Power, S., Edwards, T., Whitty, G., & Wigfall, V. (2003). *Education and the middle class*. Philadelphia: Open University Press.

Rapp, R., Ross, E., & Bridenthal, R. (1979). Examining family history. *Feminist studies*, *5*(1), 174–200.

Reimer, M. (1988). The social organization of the labour process: A case study of the documentary management of clerical labour in the public service. Unpublished dissertation, University of Toronto.

Richardson, T. R. (1989). *The century of the child: The mental hygiene movement and social policy in the United States and Canada*. Albany, NY: SUNY Press.

Riley, D. (1983). *War in the nursery: Theories of the child and mother*. London: Virago.

Rosenau, P. M. (1992). *Post-modernism and the social sciences: Insights, inroads, and intrusions*. Princeton, NJ: Princeton University Press.

Rothman, S. M. (1978). *Woman's proper place: A history of changing ideals and practices, 1870 to the present*. New York: Basic.

Roy, W. G. (1997). *Socializing capital: The rise of the large industrial corporation in America*. Princeton, NJ: Princeton University Press.

Rubin, I. I. (1973). *Essays on Marx's theory of value*. Montréal: Black Rose.

Ryan, M. (1981). *Cradle of the middle class: The family in Oneida County, New York 1790–1965*. Cambridge, MA: Cambridge University Press.

Sapoito, S., & Lareau, A. (1999). School selection as a process: The multiple dimensions of race in framing educational choice. *Social Problems*, *46*(3), 418–39.

Schiesl, M. J. (1977). *The politics of efficiency: Municipal administration and reform in America: 1880–1920*. Berkeley: University of California Press.

Schiffrin, D. (1994). *Approaches to discourse*. Oxford & Cambridge, MA: Basil Blackwell.

Schiller, H. I. (1996). *Information inequality: The deepening social crisis in America*. New York: Routledge.

Schlossman, S. L. (Fall 1981). Philanthropy and the gospel of child development. *History of Education Quarterly*, 275–99.

Schneider, B., & Coleman, J.S. (Eds.). (1993). *Parents, their children, and schools*. Boulder, CO: Westview.

Schor, J. (1992). *The overworked American: The unexpected decline of leisure.* New York: Basic.

Sewell, W. H. & Shah, V. P. (1967). Socioeconomic status, intelligence and the attainment of higher education. *Sociology of Education, 40,* 1–23.

Sharp, R., & Green, A. (1975). *Education and social control: A study in progressive primary education.* London: Routledge & Kegan Paul.

Smith, D. E. (1986). Institutional ethnography: A method of a sociology for women. *Resources for Feminist Research, 15*(1), 6–12.

———. (1987). *The everyday world as problematic: A feminist sociology.* Toronto: University of Toronto Press, & Boston: Northeastern University Press.

———. (1988a). *Sociological theory as methods of writing patriarchy into feminist texts.* Paper presented in the theory section of the American Sociological Association meetings, Atlanta.

———. (1988b). Women's work as mothers: A new look at the relations of family, class and school achievement. In G. Miller & J. Holstein (Eds.), *Perspectives on Social Problems, 1,* Greenwich, CT: JAI.

———. (1990a). *The conceptual practices of power: A feminist sociology of knowledge.* New York: Routledge, & Boston: Northeastern University Press.

———. (1990b). *Texts, facts and femininity: Exploring the relations of ruling.* London & New York: Routledge.

———. (1993). The standard North American family: SNAF as an ideological code. *Journal of Family Issues,* special issue. *14*(2), 50–65.

———. (1998). The underside of schooling: Restructuring, privatization, and women's unpaid work. *Journal for a Just and Caring Education,* special issue. *4*(1), 11–29.

———. (1999). *Writing the social: Critique, theory, and investigations.* Toronto: University of Toronto Press.

Smith, D. E., & Griffith, A. (1990). Coordinating the uncoordinated: Mothering, schooling and the family wage. In G. Miller & J. Holstein (Eds.), *Perspectives on social problems, 2,* Greenwich, CT: JAI.

Smith, D. E., Reimer, M., & Ueda, Y. (1978). *Working paper on the implications of declining enrolment for women teachers in the public elementary and secondary schools in Ontario.* Toronto: Commission on Declining School Enrolments in Ontario.

Smith, G. W. (1995). Accessing treatments: Managing the AIDS epidemic in Ontario. In M. Campbell & A. Manicom (Eds.), *Knowledge, experience, and ruling relations: Studies in the social organization of knowledge.* Toronto: University of Toronto Press.

Smith, M.L., et al. (2004). *Political spectacle and the fate of American schools.* New York: RoutledgeFalmer.

Snow, C., and Ferguson, C. (Eds.). (1977). *Talking to children: Language input and acquisition research.* Cambridge: Cambridge University Press.

St. John, E., Griffith, A., & Allen-Haynes, L. (1997). *Families in schools: A chorus of voices in restructuring.* Portsmouth, NH: Heineman.

Stevenson, D. L., & Baker, D. P. (1986). Mother's strategies for children's school achievement: Managing the transition to high school. *Sociology of Education, 59*(3), 156–66.

———. (1987). The family–school relation and the child's school performance. *Child Development, 58*(5), 1348–57.

Strasser, S. (1980). *Women and household labour.* Beverley Hills: Sage.

Strong-Boag, V. (1982). Intruders in the nursery: Child care professionals reshape the years one to five, 1920–1940. In J. Parr (Ed.), *Childhood and family in Canadian history.* Toronto: McClelland Stewart.

Sutherland, N. (1976). *Children in English Canadian society: Framing the twentieth century consensus.* Toronto: University of Toronto Press.

Thompson, E. P. (1966). *The making of the English working class.* New York: Vintage.

Ueda, Y. (1986). Japanese corporate wives in Canada: Serving the corporate order. Unpublished PhD dissertation, University of Toronto.

Valpy, M. (2 October 1993a). The 40% factor. *The Globe and Mail*, D1, 5.

Vanier Institute of the Family (2002). Profiling Canada's families. Retrieved January, 2003, from http://www.vifamily.ca

Veblen, T. (1968). *Higher learning in America*. New York: Hill & Wang.

Vincent, C. (2000). *Including parents? Education, citizenship and parental agency*. Buckingham: Open University Press.

Waite, L., & Nieken, M. (1999). *The rise of the dual career middle class family*. Alfred P. Sloan Working Families Centre, working paper, 99–101, Chicago: Center on Parents, Children and Work.

Walker, V. S. (2000). Valued segregated schools for African American children in the south, 1935–1969: A review of common themes and characteristics. *Review of Educational Research*, 70(3), 253–85.

Walkerdine, V. (1984). Developmental psychology and the child centred pedagogy. In J. Henriques, W. Holloway, C. Urwin, C. Venn, & V. Walkerdine (Eds.), *Changing the subject: Psychology, social regulation and subjectivity*. London: Methuen.

Walkerdine, V., & Lucey, H. (1989). *Democracy in the kitchen: Regulating mothers and socializing daughters*. London: Virago.

Weber, M. (1978). *Economy and society*. Berkeley: University of California Press.

Weedon, C. (1987). *Feminist practice and poststructuralist theory*. Oxford & New York: Basil Blackwell.

Weiss, N. P. (1978). The mother-child dyad revisited: Perceptions of mothers and children in twentieth-century child-rearing manuals. *Journal of Social Issues*, 34(2), 29–45.

Wesolowski, W., & Wesolowski, S. (1994). Class. In W. Outhwaite & T. Bottomore (Eds.), *The Blackwell dictionary of twentieth-century social thought*. Oxford: Blackwell.

Wilson, E. (1977). *Women and the welfare state*. London: Tavistock.

Wilson, W. J. (1987). *The truly disadvantaged: The inner city, the underclass, and public policy*. Chicago: University of Chicago Press.

Winter, J. (1997). *Democracy's oxygen: How corporations control the news*. Montréal: Black Rose.

Winters, W. G. (1993). *African American mothers and urban schools: The power of participation*. New York & Toronto: Lexington Books & Maxwell Macmillian.

Wolpe, A. M. (1978). Education and the sexual division of labour. In A. Kuhn & A. M. Wolpe (Eds.), *Feminism and materialism*. London: Routledge & Kegan Paul.

Wright, E. O. (1985). *Classes*. London: Verso.

Young, R. (Ed.). (1981). *Untying the text: A poststructuralist reader*. London: Routledge.

Index

A

academic achievement *See* achievement
academic background of parents, 5, 116–17, 118, 119, 122, 125, 131–2, 135
accumulation *See* regime
achievement: academic, 10, 14 , 38, 40, 63, 71, 114–15, 117, 120–1, 125
 class and academic, 15–6, 24, 26–7, 38, 65, 125
 See also report cards
Acker, J., 16
activism: of women, 22–3, 23–4, 138n10
administrators: and discourse, 34
 interviews with, 8, 47, 57, 60–2, 107–9, 118, 131
 and neighborhood changes, 117, 131
 work of, 8, 11, 10–9, 107–9, 126
advice columns, 37, 38, 41, 44
African-North Americans, 22–3, 138n6
 activism of, 23–4
 See also black
agency, 15–16, 28, 29
 and the ruling relations, 18, 23, 28
 See also subjectivity
Ames, Bill (father), 81, 101, 102, 138n2
Ames, Sally (mother), 81–2, 85, 101
Anna (mother), 135
anxiety, 31–3, 39, 72, 124, 134
Apple, Janie (mother), 43, 53, 58, 59, 64
apprenticeship, 18

area superintendent, 5–6
Arnup, K., 39
assistant superintendents, 107, 120–1
Australia, 128
authorities, 37, 39–40, 124
 male, 129
 See also mothering discourse

B

"baby gurus," 38
"bad mothering moment," 48
Baker, Astrid (mother), 51, 56, 58–9
Bakhtin, M.M., 33
behavior: "good entry," 7, 116–17, 118
 as mothers' responsibility, 35, 39, 40, 129
 problem, 109, 119, 129
 See also problem children
Bettelheim, B., 38
black: families, 129
 neighborhoods, 108
 women and credentials, 24
 See also African-North Americans
blaming the mother, 38, 39
books *See* child rearing texts
Bourdieu, P., 15
Bowlby, J., 38
bourgeoisie, 16
 new petty, 21
 petite, 137n1

See also middle class; new middle class; old middle class

Britain, 16, 38

British Columbia, 135

"broken homes," 109
   See also single-parent families

Brown, A., 39

budgets: of school, 65, 133
   See also funding

bureaucracy, 17–19, 22, 65

C

Canada, 19, 24, 39, 48, 128, 130–1, 134

capital, 21
   cultural, 15, 28

capitalism, 10, 16
   as organization, 20–1, 127–8

capitalist class, 137n2

Cartwright, Ellis (father), 52, 100–1, 103

Cartwright, Margaret (mother), 52–3, 86–8, 100–1, 103

careers: husbands, 25–6, 27–8, 29
   women's, 25–6, 27–8

category: of full-time housewives, 70
   of single-parent families, 108
   See also concept

Chamboredon, J.C., 138n2

Chatelaine, 39

Chicago, 122

childcare, 38, 43, 57, 97

child-centered education, 36

child development, 36–8, 39, 43, 44–5, 109
   discourse, 36–8, 44–5, 138n2
   See also psychology

child poverty *See* poverty

child psychology, 36
   See also psychology

child-rearing: books, 44, 138n8
   manuals, 34, 37
   TV programs, 44

children: academic achievement of, 10, 14, 24, 38, 71, 108
   outcomes of schooling for, 15, 108
   "problem," 1, 39, 40, 113, 115, 129
   psychological health of, 38
   school experience of, 113–14, 127
   self-management of homework by, 79, 81, 85, 91

Chile, 128

citizenship, 128

class, 9, 10, 43, 47, 137n2

and academic achievement, 15–6, 24, 26–7, 38, 65, 125

capitalist, 137n2

concept of, 14, 15–17

as coordination, 14

and curriculum, 15, 24, 122

differences, 4, 15, 20, 29, 66, 76

and discourse, 33

father's, 16

and gender, 13, 16, 22, 24, 28, 29, 138n5

"positional" concept of, 15–16

reproduction of, 9, 13, 16–7, 21–2, 23–5, 25–8, 29, 127

and social organization, 15–16, 20–1, 25, 127

and supplementary educational work, 116

under-, 129

See also middle class; new middle class; working class

classroom: routines, 10, 62
   size 109, 127, 129, 132–3

community *See* neighborhood

complementary educational work, 65–88, 89–106, 130–1
   concept of, 67
   as contribution to school 67–9
   diversified, 78–81, 97
   of employed mothers, 89–105
   of fathers, 81, 86, 98–105, 135
   and fathers' jobs, 99–100
   flexible, 81–5, 91–4
   full-time housewives', 69–88, 97
   of mothers and women, 65–6, 67–88, 89–105, 125, 130–1
   not strongly school oriented, 85–7, 94–7
   of parents, 67
   patterns of, 88
   practices of, 87–8
   as priority, 71–7
   and school operation, 67–8

concept: of class, 14, 15–17
   of complementary educational work, 67
   creation and mother's discourse, 40
   of discourse, 18, 33–5
   "expectations" as administrative, 121–2
   of the "family," 28
   of historical trajectory, 10, 126
   of labor, 123
   of the new middle class, 8, 20–1
   of new petty bourgeoisie, 21
   of "parental involvement," 14–15, 28, 108, 133

of parents for schools, 108
of regime of accumulation, 127
of the "sensitive mother," 38
of the "single parent," 138n1
of social organization, 16
of social relations, 16–17, 124
of supplementary educational work, 3
of time, 47–8
of work, 3–4, 47–8, 49, 123–4
See also category
consciousness, 18, 34
contradiction: capitalist, 20–1
between parents and appraisal, 114
coordination: of activities, 14, 16–17
family-school, 15, 64, 108, 112
of fathers-school schedules, 99–100, 103
of mothering discourse, 31, 33, 35, 37, 43
of family schedules, 10–11, 47–9, 53–5, 64, 81–2, 112, 124–5
of scheduling disjuncture, 47–9, 53–55, 63
in social sequences, 43, 124
of teachers' experience, 34
of work of professionals, 36
corporations, 17–8, 25
and restructuring, 127–8
women of, 25
Couzyn, Joanne (mother), 50–1, 59
Craft, M., 38
credentials, 17–19, 22, 126–7
and black women, 24
and white women, 25
cultural capital, 15, 28
curriculum, 10, 24, 36–7, 68, 69, 122, 127, 134–5, 139n1
and class, 15, 24, 122
delivery, 14, 60–1, 67–8
and neoconservatism, 128
and scheduling, 60–2
standardized, 17, 65, 130
standards, 133, 135
Curtis, B., 19

D

David, M., 138n10
Davidoff, L., 16, 137n5
day care centers, 54
"'defective families," 2, 38, 129
"defective mothers," 35
democracy, 131
Denmark, 128

Desmond, Martha (mother), 71–5, 76, 81, 82, 85, 90, 93, 98, 102, 105
Desmond, Ray (father), 74, 102
developmental psychology, 10, 36–8
See also child development
Dexter, Anne (mother), 44–5, 50, 57, 58
differences: class, 4, 15, 20, 29, 66. 76
between Downtown and Uptown schools, 66, 109–10, 113–16, 125–7
in educational work, 11
in parental resources, 117–18, 122, 135
between middle- and working-class schools, 5–6, 6–7, 109–10, 113–16, 126–7, 135
between public and private schools, 134–5
in orientation to mothering discourse, 43
production of, 26–7, 45
discourse: child development, 36–8, 44–5, 138n2
and class, 33
concept of, 18, 33–5
discovering, 31–5
educational, 34, 37, 40, 138n1
and morality, 33, 39–41, 42
"neoconservative," 128
public, 128, 130, 131
and subjectivity, 28
See also mothering discourse
"discursive fields," 34
Downtown School, 5–6, 47–8, 59–62, 63, 66, 69, 82–5, 89, 91–4, 98, 99–103
differences from Uptown School, 109–10, 113–16, 66, 125–7
and fathers, 99–100, 103
patterns of educational work, 104–5
principal, 61–2, 119–22
teachers, 109–16, 126
DuBois, W.E.B., 138n7

E

Ecker, Ben (father), 93, 103, 105
Ecker, Fran (mother), 93–4, 103, 105
education: child-centered, 36
discourse, 34, 37, 40, 138n1
historical trajectory of, 10, 11, 126
and racial struggle, 22–3
universal, 19, 22, 28, 40
educational discourse, 34, 37, 40, 138n1
educational equality, 65
educational experts See authorities

mothering discourse
educational policies, 107, 136
educational psychology, 1
educational reforms, 128–9
   See also restructuring
educational researchers, 15
educational routines *See* educational work
educational work, 10–11, 81, 82, 88, 122, 125,
   127, 128
  diversified, 78–81
  of fathers, 11, 89, 102, 103, 105, 138n2
  flexible, 81–5
  gender division of, 102–3
  of mothers, 26–7, 82, 88
  not strongly school oriented, 85–8
  of parents, 66–8, 70, 108–9, 122
  patterns of, 104–5
  as priority, 71–8, 90–1
  of schools, 26, 40, 43, 47, 69, 71, 122, 124,
   132–3
  See also complementary educational
   work; supplementary educational work; routines work
Ehrenreich, B. and J., 20
employment:, 7, 13, 22, 66, 67, 78, 86, 93,
   99–100, 101, 103, 105–6
  fathers', 7, 13, 22, 66, 67, 78, 86, 93,
   99–101, 103, 105–6
  mothers', 3–4, 11, 59, 63, 66–7, 69–70,
   89–106, 123
  parents', 116, 121
engine of inequality, 9, 10, 17, 24, 28, 127,
   131, 133, 136
England, 138n5
environmental influence, 36
equality: barriers to, 128–30, 130–1
  and opportunity, 9
  and neoconservatism, 129
  potential for, 127, 133
  and public education, 8–10
ethnicity, 127
  See also race
ethnography: feminist, 45–6
  institutional, 1–4, 31, 41, 45–6, 123–5
Evans, Desi (mother), 44–5, 51–52, 63
Evans, T., 129
expectations: educators', 7, 121–2
  parents', 117, 120–1, 122
  teachers', 107–8, 109–11, 120, 135
experience: of administrators, 107–8
  child's school, 113–4, 127

authors' and mothers', 1–4, 11, 13, 32, 34,
   35, 37, 38, 41
  and institutional ethnography, 1–4, 123–4
  of teachers, 34, 107–8, 114
  women's, 107, 123–4
experts, 124
  See also authorities; mothering discourse
Eyer, D.E., 38

F
families, 11
  black, 129
  categories of, 108
  achievement of, 15, 125
  as concept, 28
  coordination of school and, 15, 64, 108,
   112
  "defective," 2, 38, 129
  educational goals of, 113
  educators' characterization of, 6, 108
  female-headed, 129
  gender organization of, 14
  "imperfect," 1–2
  "intact," 38
  male-centered, 129–30
  middle-class, 9, 15, 21, 64, 98, 108–9, 130,
   133, 135, 138n5
  and neighborhood characteristics, 6, 108,
   121
  nuclear, 1, 40
  of old middle class, 21
  organization of, 40, 130–33
  routines, 10–11, 48–9, 59, 100, 105–6
  and school relations, 8, 10, 15, 47, 64,
   115–16, 122, 124–6, 136
  single-parent, 1–2, 4, 8, 13, 35, 38, 89, 91,
   108–9, 119, 121
  traditional, 123, 129
  work of, 108
  working class, 15
  work organization of, 48
  See also "standard North American family"
family routines *See* routines
family schedules, 10–11, 47–9, 53–5, 64, 81–2,
   124–5
family-school relation, 8, 10, 15, 47, 64,
   115–16, 122, 124–6, 136
  and reproduction of middle class, 13
fathering work *See* fathers

fathers: as active or interested in educational work, 103, 105
  and class, 16
  complementary educational work of, 81, 86, 98–105, 135
  Downtown School, 99–100, 103
  educational work of, 11, 89, 102, 138n2
  employment of, 7, 13, 22, 66, 67, 78, 86, 93, 99–101, 103, 105–6
  and homework, 99
  income, 9
  Uptown School, 100–103, 138n2
  See also husbands
"faulty mothering," 38
feelings See anxiety; guilt
feminism See women's movement
feminist ethnography, 45–6
  See also institutional ethnography
Fergus, Chris (husband), 86, 88, 101–2
Fergus, Patricia (mother), 85–6, 88
Fine, M., 3, 132, 133
Fisher, Marie (mother), 32–3
flexibility: in complementary educational work, 81–5, 91–4
  and educational work, 81–5
  in routines, 81–5
  of schedules, 49, 63, 89, 92, 101, 134
Fordism, 127
Foucault, M., 18, 33, 34
France, 138n2
Froebel, F., 23
full-time housewives, 11, 13, 31, 44, 49, 66, 67, 69–88, 105
  category of, 70
  complementary educational work of, 69–88, 97
  and scheduling, 49
full-time mothers, 31
funding, 11, 128–9, 132–3, 135
  See also budgeting
fundraising, 6, 79, 133

G
gender, 9
  and class, 13, 16, 22, 24, 28, 29, 138n5
  distinctions, 14
  and division of family educational work, 102–3
  organization, 9, 10, 14, 16, 22, 24, 28, 127
Globe and Mail, 48, 132–3
"good entry behavior," 7, 116–17, 118

"good mother," 39
Gordon, Alec (husband), 84, 105, 115
Gordon, Nancy (mother), 83–5, 115
Gouldner, A., 20
grandmothers, 37
Griffith, A., 1–2, 31–3, 38, 40, 41, 43, 133, 138n1
guilt, 1, 31–3, 39

H
Hall, C., 16, 137n5
Head Start (prekindergarten), 127
Heller, Susan (mother), 89, 94–6, 98
Henderson, A., 14
Higginbotham, E., 131
Hispanic peoples, 22
historical trajectory:, 10, 126
  of education, 10, 11, 126
  of inequality, 8–9, 11
  of the middle class, 14, 17, 126, 133
  of mothering for schooling, 13–14, 17–19, 29
  of the new middle class, 14, 126–7
homework, 69, 71–3, 77–82, 83–6, 90–1, 93, 94–5, 96–7, 102, 110–3, 115, 122, 125, 134–5
  children's self-management of, 79, 81, 85, 91
  and fathers, 99
  See also literacy, reading
housewives, 11, 13, 31, 44, 49, 66, 67, 69–88, 93, 97, 105
housework, 38
  as work, 10–11, 38, 41, 123
husbands, 25–6, 27–8, 29, 31, 43–45, 47, 51, 59
  income of, 26, 130
  See also fathers

I
"ideal mothers," 35
ideology 1,
  neoconservative, 35–6, 128–30, 131
  of the single parent, 8
"'imperfect" families, 1–2
inadequacy See anxiety; guilt
inequality: educational, 107
  and gender, 16
  historical trajectory of, 8–9, 11
  of opportunity, 2
  reproduction of, 4, 9, 16, 29, 108, 131, 136

and schooling, 13–14, 28, 47, 138n10
  See also engine of inequality
informal learning, 24
inner city schools, 6, 68–9, 119–122
inquiry: point d'appui of, 3
institutional ethnography: and experience,
      1–4, 123–4
  method of inquiry of, 2–3, 31, 41, 45–6,
      123–5
institutional regime, 4, 124
institutions, 4, 21, 34
  ruling, 17
"intact families," 38
intelligentsia, 20
intergenerational continuities *See* intergener-
      ational reproduction
intergenerational reproduction, 27–8, 29
  as continuity, 23–5
  and senior generations, 37
  See also reproduction
interviewing: method, 4, 31, 123, 125
  and mothering discourse, 31–3, 35, 41–6,
      124
  and relevance, 41–2
  See also interviews, institutional ethnog-
      raphy
interviews, 3, 4–5, 8, 47, 66
  with administrators, 8, 47, 57, 60–2,
      107–9, 118
  with Downtown School mothers, 7–8,
      47–8, 69–70, 82–5, 86–8, 89,
      91–4, 94–7, 98, 100–1
  with assistant superintendents, 107,
      120–1
  with educators, 31, 107–8
  in Maltby, 8
  with mothers, 7–8, 31–3, 35, 41–6, 47–8,
      107–8, 124, 133–4
  with parents, 122
  with principals, 8, 57, 61–2, 107, 116–20
  with superintendents, 8, 107
  with teachers, 8, 59–62, 107–9, 110–16,
      122
  in Turner's Crossing, 5, 47, 66, 132
  with Uptown School mothers, 7–8, 47, 54,
      69–70, 71–81, 85–6, 88, 90–1,
      98, 99, 101–6, 68–9, 119–122
  See also interviewing
involvement *See* "parental involvement"
Irwin, Carol (mother), 42, 56–7, 63–4, 89
      96–7, 98
Irwin, David (husband), 56

J
Jackson, Gerry (husband), 91–2
Jackson, Paula (mother), 48, 89, 91–3, 98, 105
Japan 138n6

K
Kanter, R.M., 25
Knight, Amanda (mother), 75–8, 81, 82, 85,
      90, 93, 98, 102, 105
Knight, Joseph (father), 102
knowledge, 19, 34, 36, 37, 40, 44
Kondos, D., 138n6
Kozol, J., 129

L
labor: concept of, 123
  See also work
Lareau, A., 3, 14, 15, 35, 65, 115–6, 122
Lawrence, A., 48–9
Lindsay, Barbara (mother), 59, 82–3
Lindsay, Mr. (father), 105
literacy, 18, 68–9, 78–9
  See also homework; reading
Louisiana, 108, 134, 135
Lowe, G., 21
Lucy, H., 38, 41
lunch programs, 50, 57
Lynd, R. and S., 37

M
Macdonnell, D., 33
magazines *See* women's magazines
Maltby, 4–5, 5–6, 8, 42, 47, 67, 107, 137n3
  changes in neighborhood, 117, 131
  interviews in, 8
  mentioned, 48, 54–5, 59, 66, 69, 71–78,
      78–81, 81–5, 85–7, 90–1, 92–4,
      95–7, 99, 120, 121
management, 17–19, 20–2
Manicom, A., 14, 67–8, 108, 122, 130, 139n1
manuals *See* child-rearing
marriage, 24, 26
Marxist theory, 137n2
Marx, K., 124, 125
mediation: and work of mothers, 107
  See also textual mediation
Mehan, H., 68
men's movements, 129–30
mental health problems, 38
mental hygiene movement, 37

method: of inquiry, 2–3, 31
  of institutional ethnography, 2–3, 31, 41,
    45–6, 123–5
  interviewing, 4, 31, 123, 125
Mexico, 138n6
middle class: British, 16
  emergence of, 16, 29
  English, 138n5
  families, 9, 15, 21, 64, 98, 108–9, 130, 133,
    135, 138n5
  fathers, 13
  French, 138n2
  gender organization of the, 13, 24
  historical trajectory of, 14, 17, 126, 133
  and Marxist theory, 137n2
  mothers, 26
  neighborhood, 4–5, 14, 44, 62, 67, 107,
    117, 125–7, 135
  parents, 65–7, 113, 116, 122, 136
  reproduction of, 13, 17, 21–2, 29, 127
  schools, 5–6, 6–7, 67–8, 107, 109–10,
    113–16, 122, 126–7, 135
  women, 10, 13–14, 22, 23–5, 36, 133, 136
  See also new middle class; old middle
    class
Mills, C.W., 20, 21
Ministry of Education (Ontario), 40
minorities, 29
  See also African-North American, black,
    race
Moore, Helen (mother), 79–81, 98–9, 105,
    138n2
Moore, Wayne (father), 79, 81, 98–9, 138n2
moral order, 26
morality: and discourse, 33, 39–41, 42
  and decline of male-headed family,
    129–30
  and "failure" of mothers, 129
mothering discourse, 8, 10, 26, 29, 31–46, 98,
    138n1
  and child development discourse, 36–8,
    44–5
  and concepts, 40
  discovery of, 33
  and interviews with mothers, 31–3, 35,
    41–6, 124
  inventing, 35–9
  moral logic of the, 39–41
  and mothering work, 39, 40–1, 43, 124,
    132
  and mother's unpaid work, 39
  and public education, 31

replaces experience of senior generation,
    37
  and the ruling relations, 28
  and standardization, 35
  and texts, 37, 40–1
  and time, 48
  and TV, 36, 44
mothering for schooling, 8, 44
  historical trajectory of, 13–14, 17–19, 29
mothering-school relation, 123–6
mothering work, 3, 7–9, 24, 59, 125–6
  authors', 1–4, 31–3, 134
  and child development discourse, 36–8,
    138n2
  defined, 10
  learnt from senior generation, 37
  and mothering discourse, 39, 40–1, 43,
    124, 132
  and poverty, 132
  and restructuring, 134–5
  and routines, 54, 71
  See also work
mothers: blaming, 38, 39
  and child's mental health, 38
  complementary educational work of,
    65–6, 67–88, 89–105, 125, 130–1
  contribution to public school system, 21
  "defective," 35
  educating, 37
  employment of, 3–4, 11, 59, 63, 66–7,
    69–70, 89–106, 123
  experience of, 1–4, 11, 13, 32, 34, 35, 37,
    38, 41
  "failure," of 129
  "faulty," 38
  full-time, 31
  "good," 39
  "ideal," 35
  informal learning of, 24
  interviews with, 7–8, 31–3, 35, 41–6,
    47–8, 107–8, 124, 133–4
  "moral failure," of 129
  and mothering discourse, 31–3, 35, 41–6,
    124
  "problem," 31, 39
  and scheduling, 47–64, 73, 105
  and schooling, 33
  and school relation, 123–6
  single, 35, 131
  as "Supermoms," 39
  supplementary educational work of, 3–4,
    9, 13, 24, 26, 44–5

and teacher relationship, 115
time of, 104
work of, 3, 7–9, 10–1, 13–4, 24, 26–7,
    31–2, 36–8, 39, 40–1, 43, 50, 54,
    64, 81, 82, 89–90, 105, 107, 108,
    124–5
    See also housewives
    interviews
    schedules
    women
movement: men's, 129–30
    mental hygiene, 37
    parent education, 36–7
    PTA, 23
    for peace and social justice, 23
    women's, 10, 25, 28, 123
    women's, suffrage 42
Murray, C., 129

N

Nancy (mother), 134
National Congress of Colored Parents and
    Teachers, 24
National Congress of Mothers, 23
National Congress of Parent-Teachers
    Associations, 23
National Population Health Survey, 131
Native peoples, 22
Naysmith, Lisa (mother), 78–81, 82, 105
Naysmith, Stuart (father), 78
neighborhood, 11
    black, 108
    changes, 7, 117, 131
    characteristics and family characteristics,
        6, 108, 121
    Downtown School, 5–6, 119–22, 125–6
    inner city, 6, 68–9, 119–122
    middle-class, 4–5, 14, 44, 62, 67, 107, 117,
        125–7, 135
    mixed, 68
    and parenting, 132
    Uptown School, 6–7, 63, 117, 125–6
    white, 108, 137n3
    working-class, 4–5, 13, 14, 62, 67, 107,
        115–16, 117, 125–7
"neoconservatism," 35–6, 128–30, 131
new familism, 130
new middle class, 20–3
    and bifurcation of women's lives, 25–6
    concept of the, 8, 20–1
    emergence of, 10

gender organization of, 22
    historical trajectory of, 14, 126–7
    reproduction of, 9, 21, 22, 24–5, 25–8
    and the ruling relations, 20, 22
    women of the, 21, 23–5, 40
new petty bourgeoisie, 21
New Zealand, 128
nuclear family, 1, 40
    See also "standard North American fam-
        ily"

O

objectification: and the ruling relations, 18
    of social relations, 16–17
old middle class, 20, 21
Ontario, 40, 49, 51, 128, 135
    government of, 133, 134
opportunity: educational, 65
    equal, 9
organization, 2, 10, 17
    capitalism as, 20–1, 127–8
    class and social, 15–16, 20–1, 25, 127
    discursive, 34–5, 46
    economic, 36, 127–8
    gender, 9, 10, 14, 16, 22, 24, 28, 127
    family, 40, 130–3
    of family's daily routine, 104
    family work, 13, 48
    of North American societies, 8
    social, 15–16, 18, 20–1, 25, 43, 65, 127
    standard family, 40
    textual, 37
Orton, Mr. (father), 105
Orton, Alice (mother), 54–5, 59, 89, 90–1,
    97–8, 105, 138n3

P

parent advisory councils, 26, 138n1
"parental influence," 129
parent education movement, 36–7
"parental involvement," 65, 69, 107–8, 110,
    116, 117–19, 125–6, 130, 132
    concept of, 14–15, 28, 108, 133
parents: academic background of, 5, 116–17,
    118, 122, 125, 131–2, 135
    complementary educational work of, 67
    and contradiction with appraisal, 114
    differences in resources of, 117–18, 122,
        135
    and educational policies, 107, 136

educational work of, 66–8, 70, 108–9, 122, 126
education movement of, 36–7
employment of, 116, 121
expectations of, 117, 120–1, 122
interviews with, 122
middle-class, 65–7, 113, 116, 122, 136
occupations of interviewed, 66
and pressure on teachers, 113–15, 126
schools' conception of, 108
single, 1–2, 4, 8, 13, 35, 38, 89, 91, 108–9, 119, 121, 138n1
supplementary educational work of, 109, 113–16, 119, 122
two, 2
working-class, 65–7, 115–16
parent-teacher associations (PTAs), 23–4, 26, 36, 79
particularized relations, 18, 37
Passeron, J. C., 15
pedagogy, 24, 36, 38, 69, 122, 127, 138n2
Pérez-Lizaur, M., 138n6
Personal Responsibility and Work Opportunities Act (1996), 131
petite bourgeoisie, 137n1
policies, 107, 136
postmodernism, 28
Poulantzas, N., 20–1, 137n1
poverty, 108, 129, 135
    child, 131–2
practices, 34–5, 65, 71, 107, 109, 115, 139n1
    of complementary educational work, 87–8
    curriculum and pedagogic, 127
prekindergarten, 127
Prevot, J., 138n2
principal: of Downtown School, 61–2, 119–22
    interviews with, 8, 57, 61–2, 107, 116–20
    on punctuality, 61–2
    Uptown School, 116–19, 122, 126
privatization, 128, 130
private schools, 134–5
problematic of the study, 41
"problem children," 1, 39, 40, 113, 115, 129
    See also behavior
"problem mothers," 31, 39
professionalization: and credentials, 17–18, 22, 126–7
    and mothering discourse, 35, 39–40
Progressive Conservative government (Ontario), 133

Promise Keepers, 129–30
psychological health, 38
psychology: developmental, 10, 36–8
    educational, 1
    See also child development
public discourse, 128, 130, 131
public education, 128, 133–5
    and equality, 8–10
    and the mothering discourse, 31
    mothers' contribution to, 21
    and reproduction of the middle class, 13
    and the ruling relations, 19, 23
    and state formation, 19
    universal, 19, 22, 28, 40, 134
public discourse, 128, 130, 131
public institutions, 128
public schools See public education
public transportation, 132
punctuality, 60–4, 69

R
race, 9, 29, 127
    and exclusion, 22–3
    and segregation, 24, 26–7
    See also blacks; whites
reading:, 26, 67–9, 70, 73–4, 77–9, 81, 84–7, 91, 93, 94–5, 97, 100–3, 110, 111–14, 135, 139n1
    bedtime, 43, 74, 91, 95, 102
    mothers', 35
    See also homework; literacy
Redbook magazine, 38
'red scare', 23
reforms: educational, 128–9
    See also restructuring
regime, 4, 124
    of accumulation, 127–30
relations: family-school, 8, 10, 13, 15, 47, 64, 115–16, 122, 124–6, 136
    mothering-school, 123–6
    objectified, 16–17
    particularized, 18
    teacher-mother, 115
    See also ruling relations, social relations
report cards, 109–10
    See also achievement
representations: of mothering, 39
    See also discourse, mothering discourse
reproduction: of class, 9, 13, 16–7, 21–2, 23–5, 25–8, 29, 127
    of inequality, 4, 9, 16, 29, 108, 131, 136

intergenerational, 27–8, 29
of middle class, 13, 17, 21–2
of new middle class, 9, 21, 22, 24–5, 25–8
See also intergenerational reproduction
researchers, 15
restructuring, 35–6, 127–8
educational, 134–5
rights, 128
Robert (father), 135
routines: before school, 51
classroom, 10, 62
daily, 49, 70, 78, 80, 84, 92, 103–4
family, 10–11, 48–9, 59, 100, 105–6
flexible, 81–5
and mothering work, 54, 71
school day, 70, 75, 77, 125
See also educational work; schedules
rules, 34, 36
ruling relations, 2–3, 17, 18–19, 26, 28, 36,
137n2
and agency, 18, 23, 28
and gender organization, 10
and the new middle class, 20, 22
and public education, 19, 23
and standardization, 19

S

Sarah (mother), 134
schedules: coordination of, 10–1, 47–9, 53–5,
64, 81–2, 99–100, 103, 112,
124–5
and curriculum, 60–2
disjunctures in, 47–9, 53–5, 63
flexibility of 49, 63, 89, 92, 101, 134
and late students, 60–2, 69
and mothers, 47–64, 73, 105
and paid work, 53–4, 56, 59, 63, 105
and punctuality, 60–3
of schools, 48–9, 51, 54, 57, 59, 60–62,
63–64
See also time
schizophrenia, 38
school board: research problems with, 4, 5,
47, 66, 124, 137n4
school budgets, 65, 133
See also funding
school day, 49–64, 70, 74, 124–5
after-, 70, 75, 92
coming home from, 59, 63, 70
and family class, 64
lunch time, 57–59, 63

morning, 49–57, 63
production of regularity of, 49–50, 56, 59,
63–4
routines, 70, 75, 77, 125
at school, 59–62
schooling: and assessment, 36, 109
historical trajectory of, 17–19
and inequality, 13–14, 28, 47, 138n10
institutional order of, 3
and middle-class families, 15
and middle-class women, 13–14, 23–5,
25–8, 98
and the mothering discourse, 31
and mothers, 33
and outcomes for children, 15, 108
parental work for, 108
and the PTA movement, 23
universalized, 19, 22, 28, 40
and women's work, 22, 45–6, 47
and working-class families, 15
See also schedules, schools
schools: and complementary educational
work, 67–9
educational objectives of, 120–1
educational work of, 26, 40, 43, 47, 69, 71,
122, 124, 132–3
inner city, 6, 68–9, 119–122
middle-class, 6–7, 67–8, 107, 122, 135
private, 134–5
public 8–10, 13, 19, 21–3, 28, 40, 128,
133–5
relations of families and, 8, 10, 13, 15, 47,
64, 115–16, 122, 124–6, 136
relations of mothers and, 123–6
as social organization, 65
suburban, 122
working class, 5–6, 6–7, 67–9, 107,
109–10, 113–16, 119–22, 126–7,
135
work of, 26, 40, 43, 47, 69, 71, 122, 124,
132–3
See also Downtown School; schedules;
schooling; Uptown School
Schor, J., 130
segregation *See* race
"sensitive mothers," 38
"separation" (Lareau), 115–16
sequences of action, 43–4, 124
single mothers, 35, 131
single-parent families, 1–2, 4, 8, 13, 35, 38, 89,
91, 108–9, 119, 121
as category, 108

concept of, 138n1
skills, 18–9, 40, 68–9, 78, 121, 131
Smith, D., 1–2, 18, 31–2, 40, 41–2
social organization:, 15–16, 18, 20–1, 25, 43, 65, 127
    and gender, 16
social relations, 2–3, 10, 13, 17, 18, 21, 25, 28, 29, 34, 43
    between families and schools, 10, 47, 124–6
    concept of, 16–17, 124
    of educational inequality, 107
    See also relations, relations of ruling
social rights, 128
sociology, 38, 45, 129
    for people, 2
    for women, 2
speech genres, 33
Spock, Dr. B., 38
sports, 71, 76, 78–9, 80, 97, 102–3
"standard North American family," 2, 9, 38, 40, 41, 123
standardization: and curriculum, 17, 65, 130, 133, 135
    and mothering discourse, 35
    of organization of schools, 130
    and professions, 17
    of public educational system, 8, 9, 24
    and the ruling relations, 19
    and testing, 118, 135
    and work, 125
standpoint, 3, 4, 9
state, 17–19, 128
    formation, 19
    welfare-, 128
stereotypes, 109, 129
students: achievement of, 10, 14 , 38, 40, 63, 71, 114–15, 117, 120–1, 125
    late, 60–2, 69
subjectivity, 2, 15–16, 18, 26, 28, 35, 42, 124
    See also agency
suburban schools, 122
superintendents, 8, 107
"Supermoms," 39
supplementary educational work: and class differences, 116
    concept of, 3
    of mothers, 3–4, 9, 13, 24, 26, 44–5
    of parents, 109, 113–16, 119, 122
    and teachers, 14, 121–2

T

teachers: at Downtown School, 59–60, 62, 109–16, 126
    expectations of parental involvement, 107–8, 109–11, 120, 135
    experience of, 107–8, 114
    interviews with, 8, 59–62, 107–9, 110–16, 122
    and mothers relationship, 115
    parental pressure on, 109, 113–15, 126
    and parents' work, 109
    on punctuality, 61–2
    and supplementary educational work, 14, 121–2
    and time, 69, 122, 133
    at Uptown School, 59–60, 109–18, 125–6
    work of, 8, 11, 14, 60, 67, 69, 107–9, 121, 130–1, 133
television See TV
testing, 118, 135
texts, 18, 34–5, 37, 40–1
    objectifying, 17
textual mediation, 18, 21, 34–5, 36–7
time, 31–2, 56, 60, 62, 63, 69, 97, 116, 122, 124, 125–6
    for complementary educational work, 72, 75, 130–1
    concept of, 47–8
    and housewives, 70
    mothers', 104
    parents, 132
    and punctuality, 60–3
    teachers and, 69, 122, 133
    See also schedules
Toronto, 41, 48
traditional family, 123, 129
Turner's Crossing, 4–5, 5–6, 8, 43–4, 47, 63, 66, 107, 124, 132
    research problems in, 4, 5, 47, 66, 124, 137n4
TV, 18, 32, 56, 71, 72, 80, 81, 82, 84, 97
    and mothering discourse, 36, 44

U

unions, 65, 128
United Kingdom, 128
United States, 19, 23–4, 37, 128–9, 130–1, 132
    See also Louisiana
universal public education, 19, 22, 28, 40
unpaid work, 3–4, 9, 10, 11, 13, 28, 31, 39, 41, 66, 67, 98, 127, 128

Uptown School, 5, 6–8, 47, 54, 59–62, 63–4,
    66–7, 69–82, 81–2, 85–6, 90–1,
    98–103
  differences from Downtown School,
    109–10, 66, 113–16, 125–7
  fathers, 100–103, 138n2
  and parental involvement, 117–19, 125–6
  patterns of educational work, 104–5
  principal, 116–19, 122, 126
  teachers, 109–16, 125–6
US Department of Education, 130

V

vice principal: in Maltby, 107
  Uptown School, 60–1
volunteering, 26, 44, 133

W

Wages for Housework, 3–4, 123
Walkerdine, V,. 38, 41, 138n9
Wall Street Journal, 129
Washington, Mrs., 131
Weber, M., 17
welfare, 131
  state, 128
whites, 25
  and class reproduction, 17, 22, 24, 25,
    27–8, 29
  neighborhood of, 108, 137n3
Wilson, W.J., 129
women: activism of, 22–2, 23–4, 138n10
  agency of, 28
  careers of, 25–6, 27–8
  complementary educational work of,
    65–6
  "of the corporation," 25
  experience of, 107, 123–4
  income of, 130
  learning from, 45
  married, 130
  middle class, 10, 13–14, 22, 23–5, 36, 127,
    133, 136
  of the new middle class, 21, 23–5, 40
  sociology for 2
  supplementary educational work of, 3–4,
    9, 13, 24, 26, 44–5
  unpaid work of, 3–4, 9, 10, 11, 13, 28, 31,
    39, 41, 66, 67, 98, 127, 128, 130
  white, 25
  work of, 16, 22, 40, 45–6, 47–48, 63, 65–7,
    98, 127, 130

women's magazines, 35, 37, 38, 39, 44
women's movement, 10, 25, 28, 123
work, 17, 53–4
  of administrators, 8, 11, 10–9, 107–9, 126,
    131
  complementary educational, 65–88,
    89–106
  concept of, 3–4, 47–8, 49, 123–4
  educational, 10–11, 81, 82, 88, 122, 125,
    127, 128
  of family, 108
  of fathers, 7, 9, 11, 13, 22, 66, 67, 78, 81,
    86, 89, 93, 98–105, 103, 105–6,
    135, 138n2
  hours, 130
  housework as, 10–11, 38, 41, 123
  and lower-income groups, 13–14
  managerial, 19
  of middle-class women, 13–14, 127
  of mothers, 3, 7–9, 10–1, 13–4, 24, 26–7,
    31–2, 36–8, 39, 40–1, 43, 50, 54,
    64, 81, 82, 89–90, 105, 107, 108,
    124–5
  parents' educational, 66–8, 70, 108–9,
    122, 126
  processes, 65
  of professionals, 36
  schedules and paid, 53–4, 56, 59, 63, 105
  of schools, 26, 40, 43, 47, 69, 71, 122, 124,
    132–3
  and standardization, 125
  supplementary educational 3–4, 9, 13, 14,
    24, 26, 44–5 109, 113–16, 119,
    121–2
  of teachers, 8, 11, 14, 60, 67, 69, 107–9,
    121, 130–1, 133
  of women, 16, 22, 40, 45–6, 47–48, 63,
    65–7, 98, 127, 130
  women's unpaid, 3–4, 9, 10, 11, 13, 28, 31,
    39, 41, 66, 67, 98, 127, 128, 130
  See also mothering work
working class, 29
  and exclusion, 22
  families, 15
  and Marxist theory, 137n2
  neighborhood, 4–5, 13, 14, 44, 66, 67,
    107, 115–16, 117, 125–7
  parents, 65–7, 115–16
  schools, 5–6, 6–7, 67–9, 107, 109–10,
    113–16, 119–22, 126–7, 135
Wright, E.O., 137n2